OPENING SPACES

OPENING SPACES

Critical Pedagogy and Resistance Theory in Composition

Joe Marshall Hardin

State University of New York Press

Published by
State University of New York Press, Albany

© 2001 State University of New York
All rights reserved.

Printed in the United States of America

For information, address State University of New York Press,
90 State Street, Suite 700, Albany, NY, 12207

Production by Christine L. Hamel
Marketing by Fran Keneston

Library of Congress Cataloging-in-Publication Data

Hardin, Joe Marshall, 1953-
    Opening spaces: critical pedagogy and resistance theory in
    composition / Joe Marshall Hardin.
        p. cm.
    Includes bibliographical references and index.
    ISBN 0-7914-4903-3 (hc: alk. paper)—
    ISBN 0-7914-4904-1 (pbk: alk. paper)
1. English Language—Rhetoric—Study and teaching. 2. English
Language—Rhetoric—Study and teaching—Political aspects. 3.
Criticism—Authorship—Study and teaching. 4. Critical thinking—Study and teaching. 5. Academic writing—Study and
teaching. I. Title.

PE1404.H362 2001

808'.042'071—dc21   00040020
                                                      CIP

10   9   8   7   6   5   4   3   2   1

Contents

Acknowledgments

Much has happened since I began to research and write this book. I hope I have grown as a teacher and as a scholar, and if I have, it is in some part due to the relationships (face-to-face and on-line) I have formed in the past few years with compositionists all over the country.

In particular, I would like to thank Gary Olson, Lynn Worsham, Tom Ross, Debra Jacobs, and Valerie Allen for their responses to this manuscript in an earlier form. Without their help, this book could not have been completed. I would especially like to thank the folks at SUNY Press, the English faculty and staff at the University of South Florida, the Language and Communication faculty and staff at Northwestern State University of Louisiana, and the faculty and staff at St. Petersburg Jr. College (Tarpon Campus). Nothing matters more than having good colleagues.

The people who work in rhetoric and composition are a unique group. At conferences and online, they have been open and willing to share their opinions, ideas, and research with me, and this openness has helped to make this book better. Generally, I find that the folks in rhetoric and composition really believe that research should be a productive conversation among scholars, and their commitment to this idea has made me feel as though my contribution, humbly submitted, will be seriously considered. This is the best thing a writer can hope for: an attentive, dedicated, informed audience.

In particular, I would like to thank Sid Dobrin, Julie Drew, Raúl Sánchez, Merry Perry, Tom West, Andrea Greenbaum, Irene Ward, Todd Taylor, Susan Miller, Colleen Connolly, Janice Walker, Priscilla Ross, Steve Brown, Christian Weisser, Lynn Stratton, Charla Bauer, Judi Isaksen, Joyce Karpay, Paul Chambers, Bonnie Kyburz, Tom Peele,

Michael Mann, and Rick MacDonald. I would also like to thank Ray and Susan Wallace for their friendship, and Linda Yakle and Sandra Kerns for their early encouragement.

Lastly, I would like to thank my parents for their belief and support, and, most of all I would like to thank my wife, Susan, for constantly asking me, "aren't you supposed to be writing?"

Introduction

> The challenge lies in conceiving of the time of political
> action and understanding as opening up a space that can
> accept and regulate the differential structure of the mo-
> ment of intervention without rushing to produce a unity
> of the social antagonism or contradiction. This is a sign
> that history is happening.
>
> (Bhabha, *The Location of Culture* 25)

Like many baby-boomers, I've often found my own sympathies aligned with ideas and movements that can only be called "resistant." For example, in the late 1960s and early 70s I was among a great many Americans who, through a sense of moral and political outrage or through a healthy regard for our own futures, resisted the Vietnam War and the draft. In fact, I can probably date my first act of overt political resistance to 1970, when I registered for the draft as a conscientious objector—a status that, I am glad to report, I never had to prove. Later, I found myself once again aligned with the forces of cultural and social resistance when I joined those who were swept up in the beginnings of the American environmental movement. While I would probably hesitate to call myself a political activist, I've more often than not found a way to identify myself with some movement that has as its founding principle a resistance to the acceptance and inevitability of institutional, cultural, or social values. To be honest, my own view of myself has largely been that I *generally* stand in resistance to the inevitability of society's institutions and values. I'd

1

like to think that this tendency is more than just egotistical contrarianism, but I suspect that there may be a bit of that involved, too. More likely, my own historical and personal context—as an American, as a baby-boomer, and as one who is generally drawn to the artistic side of human endeavor—have all combined to construct a personality that sees itself in resistance to the certainty of dominant and mainstream social and cultural values.

Whatever its source, the impulse toward resistance is also at least partially what led me to the English department. Even in the environment of my middle class, predominantly white, affluent high school, my English teachers always seemed to be the ones who most shared my sense that the values of culture and society did not have to be accepted blindly. These teachers were interested in Shakespeare and comma splices to be sure, but they were also interested in popular culture and individual self-expression. My English classes were almost invariably places where there was at least the chance of music and poetry, and the poetry was just as likely to come from a *The Beatles* or from a *Simon and Garfunkle* album as it was to come from a textbook. The discipline of English seemed to be the one place in school where resistance and idealism were welcomed. At any rate, when it came time to align myself permanently with some disciplinary study, it seemed natural to choose the English department. In my experience, English seemed to be the one discipline whose practitioners were most open to the idea that there might be an opposition to the blind acceptance of society's values. I guess that I ran into my share of overly didactic grammarians and inflexible literary pedagogues among the poetry lovers and the romantic idealists (still do), but for me, at least, the English department seemed to be the place where the cultural misfit could find some acceptance. More importantly, it seemed to be the place where those who resisted the notion that society's values are absolute and inevitable congregated.

Once I began to study rhetoric and composition, I quickly recognized again the impulse toward ideological resistance in the writings of James Berlin, Ira Shor, Patricia Bizzell, C.H. Knoblauch, Henry Giroux, and others. These folks, I soon learned, practiced a loosely aligned method of teaching called *critical pedagogy*. I think that all of these scholars would generally agree that students should be taught the skills needed to write and read within the standard conventions of cultural and academic discourses, but what sets them apart is that they also insist that students should be taught to interrogate, critique, and in some cases *resist* the values promoted by those same discourses.

I soon learned that, as with any resistance movement, there is considerable opposition to teaching critical pedagogy. In this case, there are certainly a great many who have suggested that compositionists should concern themselves exclusively with supplying students with the skills necessary to succeed in the academy and in the current economy, and that teaching students to question or to resist the values promoted and inscribed in various discourses is not a productive or an appropriate activity for the writing classroom. Whatever the nature of the criticism, there is no question that critical pedagogy and resistance theory as educational methodologies are controversial. Mark Hurlbert and Michael Blitz, in *Composition and Resistance*, construct this controversy as a basic disagreement over the obligations and responsibilities of the composition teacher:

> A great many composition educators say that it is our obligation to teach students to write and read for and within curricula made by academics for academics. Others would say that our responsibility is to assist students in resisting these constraints. The former position is, for example, the traditional objective for conservative writing across the curriculum programs. The latter view is, or perhaps has become, the definition of a critically (self-)conscious liberal education. (42)

While disputes about the goals of writing pedagogy are rarely this neatly drawn, there are clearly those who worry that critical pedagogy, and especially the teaching of *resistance*, is a futile or ethically suspect activity that should not be a primary concern of the composition classroom.

In his last book James Berlin calls for a writing classroom that is the "site of political activity and struggle," occupied by a teacher who is to serve as a "transformational intellectual" by applying a classroom method that teaches students to "negotiate and resist semiotically enforced cultural codes" (121). In a response to Berlin that appeared in *JAC: A Journal of Composition Theory*, Susan Miller illustrates just two concerns that some have about Berlin's version of critical pedagogy. She worries that such practice infantalizes students by assuming their cultural naivete, and that critical pedagogy, no matter how well-intentioned, may unfairly endorse the teacher's or the institution's ideological perspective:

It is not obvious to me that institutional claims to teach a
universal moral sense should supplant families, regional cus-
toms, class, or ethnic politics, to normalize and covertly coerce
conscience, nor that institutions can or should install a universal vision of "democratic" subjectivity. (498)

Further, Miller argues that critical pedagogy such as that espoused by
Berlin is more appropriate to the teaching of textual interpretation and
reading and not to rhetorical production and the teaching of writing:

By teaching texts rather than their making, by teaching awareness rather than rhetoric, and by teaching the power of mean-
ings rather than the making of statements, we inadvertently
reproduce a politics that is aware but passive. (499)

While Miller finally professes to share many of the same goals as
Berlin, she does raise some serious questions about the nature and
interests of critical pedagogy and about the ways students are taught
to resist in the classroom. Such questions deserve serious consideration by scholars of critical pedagogy and by those who promote the
teaching of resistance, and this book is in part an attempt to address
some of these questions.

In fact, while there may be almost tacit agreement now among
many critical teachers that teaching writing is a "political" activity,
that agreement has not made the goals or methods of the writing
classroom universally apparent, especially regarding how much political work can and should be attempted by the composition teacher.
For example, Evan Watkins agrees that teaching writing is a political
activity and that composition teachers are uniquely positioned to
promote resistance, but Watkins also warns that those committed to
teaching resistance face a "peculiar trap." According to Watkins, if
those who work in English studies hope to extend their work of
promoting resistance much beyond the confines of the classroom,
then the

education in resistance and positional struggles it affords must
begin as an education for us, in recognizing and encouraging
very different practices of resistance as they exist in other
conditions of work. (27)

Thus, if many agree that composition is the site within the academy
where politics and resistance most often are at issue, not many agree

that those issues can be addressed effectively. Along with Miller's worries that critical pedagogy infantalizes students, promotes the teacher's or the institution's ideological perspective, and favors reading over writing, such diverse scholars as Stuart Hall and Stanley Fish have worried that critical pedagogy is in danger of losing its usefulness as it becomes institutionalized. Fish writes that critical pedagogy may be merely a dangerous new "modification" to the subject of English studies based on "the lure of political hope" (101).

As one who has always been committed to that part of English studies that embraces resistance, I have written this book in order to address some of these key challenges to critical pedagogy and the teaching of resistance. In addition, I hope to help establish a more clear historical context for critical pedagogy and to suggest some new directions for those who are committed to teaching resistance. For this project, teaching resistance will be defined as critical activity that promotes resistance to the unconscious reification of ideological values as they are encountered in text, and as rhetorical production that is informed by a conscious understanding of the links between language and ideology, between rhetorical production and the in-scription of values, and between linguistic and textual representation and power. Throughout, I will argue that teaching resistance as a part of writing instruction is, in fact, an ethical and necessary activity— one that empowers students to articulate their own values through the conventions of cultural, academic, and disciplinary rhetoric once those conventions are demonstrated to be powerful, available, and useful. I will also argue that such activity can protect the autonomy of both student and teacher positions and that teaching resistance in the composition classroom can offer students the power of rhetoric without endorsing a specific set of values, other than the view that language, discourse, and rhetoric are always interested and always value-laden. Finally, I will argue that teaching resistance can focus the work of the writing classroom on rhetoric and production and can promote the articulation of student voices *if* it moves beyond the need to see itself as the emancipator of students and *if* it can encourage students to appropriate and use the rhetoric and conventions of academic and cultural discourses to inscribe their own values.

Chapter One begins by retracing some of the historical circum-stances that have made composition a politicized site. Along with Miller, Berlin, and Watkins, I argue that composition has often been made to compensate for inequalities and changes in the socio-political and cultural makeup of society, and that this has served to politicize the teaching of composition from its inception. Nevertheless, power relations in composition have never been clearly defined, and the subject matter, content, and goals of the critical composition classroom have never been sufficiently established. I contend that these ambiguities about who holds power in the writing class at least partially fuel the current debate over the goals and content of writing instruction. This chapter includes a discussion of how those who work in English studies have come to view cultural and aesthetic values in the past two centuries, and how this view of the relationship between these two sets of values influences current disciplinary practices.

In Chapter Two, I begin with an outline of reproductive theories of education, which propose that cultural values are reproduced through educational practices, and examine how resistance theories of education grew from reproductive theories. I argue that teaching resistance does not mean that compositionists have a mandate to promote specific values, nor does it mean that they must ask students to resist or accept any specific ideology. In this section, I argue that critical pedagogy only encourages students to resist the uncritical acceptance of ideological values and to view disciplinary, cultural, and academic discourses as open and available spaces wherein student writers may establish their own positions as authors and where they may learn to examine and articulate their own ideological perspectives. With Hurlbert and Blitz, I argue that teaching resistance means teaching that disciplinary, academic, and cultural discourses are not to be presented as cohesive, static, or closed systems. Instead, the rhetorical conventions of these discourses should be promoted as available and useful to a variety of subject positions. Additionally, I argue that resistance should involve teaching students that establishing their own negotiated positions within academic or cultural discourse is a process of accepting or resisting values as they are reinscribed through language and text.

In this section I also argue that teaching resistance does not promote the teacher's or the institution's values over the student's, as some compositionists have suggested, nor does it necessitate the construction of an ideal model of "correct" student reaction or a prescribed model of resistance. As many who employ critical pedagogy have noted, students will frequently choose to reject the authority of the teacher's often liberal position and espouse or express more mainstream or conservative values. But this is not at odds with teaching resistance as defined in this project. Teaching resistance requires only two specific outcomes: one, that students learn to resist the uncritical acceptance of cultural representations and institutional practices by interrogating rhetoric to uncover its motives and values; and two, that students learn to produce text that uses rhetoric and convention to give voice to their own values and positions.

Chapter Three examines how postmodern ethics and contemporary language theory further demand that writing instruction be made to address social, political, and economic issues, at least as they relate to language and rhetoric. I contend that renewed attempts to steer an ideologically neutral or disinterested course for rhetoric and writing instruction are misguided. The postmodern view of ethics insists that axiomatic and systematic ethics are of decreased use in contemporary global institutions of culture, society, and business. Now, a multiplicity of voices from a variety of cultural backgrounds are often found grappling for representation and economic power, and composition teachers must be charged with making rhetoric available to this multitude of voices. Successful writing instruction should encourage students to construct their own subject positions and motives for writing, and contemporary language theories suggest that textual production and reception are inexorably bound up with questions of ideological conflict. As such, I hope to reinforce the conclusion that separating the teaching of rhetoric and convention from considerations of ideology and value is artificial and perhaps even unethical, as that separation promulgates a discourse that promotes either cultural and academic assimilation or exclusion.

Many objections to teaching resistance in the writing classroom have come from those who question whether compositionists can introduce questions of ideology and value with an appropriate regard for students' right to their own values and opinions, or whether the power of the teacher and the academy will always subvert the right of the student to hold contrary opinions. In Chapter Four, I posit that teaching resistance is an activity that respects and empowers students if it discloses the interestedness of all parties and if it encourages students to hold, accept, or resist the values inscribed in language according to their own cultural, ethical, or moral perceptions. Teaching resistance only demands that students learn to resist the uncritical acceptance of the ideological values promoted by various discourses and their rhetoric, and to express their own values in the production of rhetorically powerful texts. This chapter also examines the composition teacher's relationship with the academy, and how the teacher's resistance to the reinscription of cultural values allows him or her to model and to promote resistance.

Finally, I argue that critical pedagogy reaffirms that education, and especially language instruction, has worked as a part of the project to advance Western culture. This is an important admission for this project's argument because knowledge of this "colonizing" impulse, which constructs the student as an object of the normalizing and nationalizing forces of the educational system, makes writing instruction and its power relations available to new elements of social theory. These elements will be used to argue that while students work to produce their own texts within academic, disciplinary, and cultural conventions, they also are engaged in a negotiated resistance to those discourses through a productive process of rearticulation and hybridization. Homi Bhabha describes this process of hybridization as "a partial and double force that is more than the mimetic but less than the symbolic . . . that turn[s] the gaze of the discriminated back upon the eye of power" (34-35). Even as students learn to use rhetoric to mimic discourse models, their own texts rearticulate that rhetoric and promote an inherent resistance to the uncritical acceptance of ideological values. Students' hybrid texts reveal the open and rhetorical nature of discourse conventions, the usefulness and strength of academic, disciplinary, and cultural rhetoric and conventions, and the openness and availability of these discourses.

In Chapter Five, I present some of the current major critiques of critical pedagogy and examine how those discussions lead away from what I think are the best lines of advance for critical pedagogy and resistance theories. Instead of defending critical pedagogy that is aligned with Freirean and liberatory practices, I argue for a renewed examination of the basic goals of critical pedagogy and resistance theories, which have been traditionally outlined as liberatory projects. Again, I argue that the key to achieving a workable critical and resistant pedagogy is to emphasize student authority and to de-emphasize the liberatory aspects of critical work.

Critical teaching and resistance are more than ways to promote critical interpretation and the liberation of students from ideological formulations—they are also ways to encourage students to write texts that contribute to current academic, disciplinary, and mainstream culture through the authoritative use of appropriated, hybridized rhetoric. Teaching resistance does not imply the overthrow or neglect of academic or disciplinary discourse conventions or rhetoric; nor does it suggest that we need to make the writing classroom a hyper-politicized place where teacher or institutional concerns overwhelm student autonomy in an attempt to create a liberated subject. Instead, by revealing that academic, disciplinary, and cultural discourses are available and open spaces and by supporting the hybridization and rearticulation of their rhetoric and conventions, critical teachers can find a way to empower and encourage student authority.

With this project, I find myself once again aligned with the forces of resistance. As such, I resist the idea that compositionists must turn away from pedagogies that openly address how language promotes ideology or constructs knowledge. Compositionists cannot be afraid to teach students to express their own values and ideas in the rhetoric of academic, cultural, or disciplinary discourses and to resist the unthinking acceptance of the values these discourses promote. With new direction, composition may yet become a place where students learn to articulate and examine their own subjectivities through powerful and authentic rhetoric—if those of us who embrace resistance as it is expressed in critical pedagogy have the courage to teach students to resist seeing academic and cultural discourses as neutral, closed places, and if we resist the notion that our pedagogy can somehow liberate our students.

For those who are looking for programmatic advice on how to implement these ideas into their own classroom activities I must present a warning: my intention is not to describe ways that these theories might be enacted in specific classroom practices. Instead, my hope is to provide compositionists who are interested in critical pedagogy with a clear understanding of how resistance theory became an issue and to suggest new directions for their own theorizing. This book is, above all, a book about how we theorize the writing class-room. My foremost belief is that teachers teach best when their own theorizing guides their classroom activities and not when they follow someone else's program, and, as such, I have tried to provide an overview of the theories that have guided critical pedagogy without prescribing specific practices. To some, much of this theorizing may seem like old ground. Still, I have never seen a clear articulation of the relationships among modern aesthetics, reproductive theories of edu-cation, resistance theory, and postmodern ethics in one place. This is, above all, what I hope to provide in the first four chapters. I do call, all the way through the text, for an increased awareness of how student texts might be seen in a new way, and I do make some brief suggestions as to how this might be accomplished. Nevertheless, my hope is that teachers and scholars who read the book will come away with new ideas about classroom practice and about critical pedagogy. Most importantly, I hope the book will suggest new directions for theorizing about critical pedagogy and resistance theories in composition.

Chapter One

English Studies, Aestheticism, and the Art-Culture System

Recent questions concerning the disciplinary status and identity of the English department have provoked a great deal of scholarship on the history of English as an academic area of study. Generally, these chronicles proceed to a similar conclusion: that the discipline of English, at least as it has been constructed since the late nineteenth century, is in an ongoing state of crisis about its subject and method.[1] As Sidney I. Dobrin notes in his review of several of these histories, "the quest for identity has become the central mission of contemporary English Departments" (692).

While this chapter is in part an attempt to contribute to this area of scholarship, I would not presume that by offering a new reading of history I might suggest what the "true nature" of contemporary English studies should be. Instead, I only want to expand the framework of these historical discussions by situating them within a larger dialogue that concerns English studies' role in the process of acculturating students. My hope is that pedagogy within reading and writing classes can be made more productive after a thorough examination of the way in which scholars in English studies have deployed particular concepts of art and culture in order to evaluate texts and cultural activity.[2]

My primary purpose is to reinforce the idea that pedagogical methods within reading and writing classes do, in fact, benefit from the study of how linguistic convention and textual representation inscribe cultural values. My thesis is that pedagogy in the writing class might be made even more productive by emphasizing the student's productive role as "author." Specifically, this chapter examines just how constructions of art and culture, as they have been theorized by scholars and teachers of English studies, have been used to split human activity into "high" and "low" categories and to make both categories submit to the critical gaze of the literary critic. The chapter considers three primary ways that scholars have theorized the concept of culture as it relates to the discipline of English, and suggests why these positions have produced mostly anxiety and ambiguity about the connection between English studies and the social project to acculturate students.[3] In this analysis, I attempt to show how these theories about the nature and meaning of art and culture have contributed to the misgivings of scholars and teachers over the future of English studies, and I undertake to reinforce the understanding that the institutional work of English studies has always been to inscribe and promote cultural value. Finally, I argue that the role of classroom writing instruction in the current "culture crisis" should be threefold: to further politicize the teaching of academic rhetoric, canon, genres, conventions, and methods; to make those forms and conventions available sites for student articulation; and to make the critical position of author a realistic possibility for students.

Crisis

One does not have to work long in higher education to become sensitized to the word "crisis," and this is especially true for those of us who work in English studies. Every passing year brings some new "crisis of education" that demands reconsideration of the goals and missions of the American system of higher education. In fact, it sometimes seems that no discipline has been presented with more of these crisis situations than has English studies. Sometimes these crises originate from changes in the national political climate, which can drastically alter popular or institutional expectations of what English studies can or should accomplish, and sometimes they arise from philosophical, political, or economic shifts within the academy or the department. Whatever its source, the need for altering or rethinking the methods and subject matter of English departments is almost always presented as a crisis situation that demands immediate and radical action.

One could argue that over the years these crises have, in fact, produced some significant changes in the way work is done in English studies, but most often, when the crisis has passed, it is just as likely that more questions have been raised than have been answered. For example, there has been a burgeoning notion among some scholars and teachers that policies and practices within English studies have too often participated in the maintenance of a social system that has excluded people from various ethnic, class, and gender groups. This exclusion, it is reasoned, has kept members of these groups from acquiring adequate representation in social, economic, and political institutions. To some, this suggests that the best course for English studies is to make retribution for its part in this injustice by promoting the study of texts and genres from other cultures. This attitude is expressed in Homi Bhabha's call for a "worlding" of literature:

> There may be a sense in which world literature could be an emergent prefigurative category that is concerned with a form of cultural dissensus and alterity, where non-consensual terms of affiliation may be established on the grounds of historical trauma. The study of world literature might be the study of the way in which cultures recognize themselves through their projections of "otherness." Where, once, the transmission of national traditions was the major theme of a world literature, perhaps we can now suggest that transnational histories of migrants, the colonized, or political refugees—these border and frontier conditions—may be the terrains of world literature. (12)

While opening new "terrains" of literature has done much to make representation in the canon available to formerly marginalized or excluded writers and their texts, it also has been a painful adjustment for the discipline of English studies. After all, it can be argued that the traditional canon has been the department's primary source of cohesion until now.

Whether moves to expand the canon have done much to alleviate the suffering of dominated or excluded peoples is debatable, but there is no doubt that the former nature of English studies has been seriously challenged by the expansion of the already over-crowed canon. In order to make room for Amy Tan, Mike Rose, Frederick Douglass, and

Aphra Behn, students necessarily get less Yeats, Dryden, Keats, and Shakespeare. While some may consider that the need to expand the canon is fairly obvious, a closer look at recent criticism reveals that the subject is far from settled, and some very good and very progressive scholars still feel adrift in the newly expanded canon.

For example, one of my colleagues told me recently that she feels she has no way to teach her students to evaluate the "goodness" of literature anymore. She's afraid to spend too much time on Shakespeare in her introductory literature classes or to tell her students that she believes Shakespeare to be "the best writer in the English language," even though she absolutely believes in the truth of that statement. While she told me that she valued the inclusion of other "marginalized" texts herself—she had never read Mike Rose before—and she welcomes the chance to make women and students from various ethnic and national origins more at home in her class, she wonders how much the inclusion of these texts does to make the short time she has with her students "more fair." I do not want to appear critical of my colleague's concerns. I think they are, instead, merely indicative of the sense of loss that some very sensitive and caring teachers feel about the expansion of the canon. More importantly, her fear about involving her students in what she calls "the aesthetic evaluation of literature" points directly, I think, to changes brought about by the influence of postructuralism, which suggests that the mission to sort the world of texts and genres into "high" and "low" categories is based on arbitrary and prejudicial structures that are, at best, only internally cohesive.

Like most Western humanist projects, we scholars in English studies have had to face the troubling realization that our ideas about what we do when we teach our students to read literature and to appreciate a well-turned metaphor have been, at times, a bit overblown. The modern project of teaching people to read and write in the Western humanist tradition no longer seems to hold the promise of saving Western civilization from the barbarians and the philistines. As Lyotard writes, "there is no longer a horizon of universalization, of general emancipation before the eyes of postmodern man" (171) that might be attained by reading great literature.

While these crises and the reactions they produce are never simple to describe, it might be said that another familiar example occurred when changes in the American economy in the last half of this century helped bring about open admissions to higher education, which precipitated the crisis of increased diversity in the classroom. Again, many English departments responded to this crisis by further expanding the coverage of their literature sections to include formerly excluded or unrecognized literatures and genres. As more women, minorities, and members of the working class began showing up in writing classes, teachers there were also compelled to increase their tolerance of individual and cultural differences in academic writing. In order to accommodate these new students in the composition class, teachers have had to accept a wider variety of influences from various cultures on individual expression, and theories have had to be expanded to examine how (and if) women and students from various class and ethnic backgrounds write and read differently. Terry Dean writes that,

> with increasing cultural diversity in classrooms, teachers need to structure learning experiences that both help students write their way into the university and help teachers learn their way into student cultures. (23)

Inevitably, the move to respond to cultural difference in the writing class has resulted in some changes in what can be considered acceptable in academic writing. These changes, coupled with the expansion of the canon, helped bring about a backlash in the 1980s—the so-called literacy crisis—which resulted in a call from some scholars and teachers (and more politicians) for the English department to return to the traditional canon of literature and to teaching basic writing skills.

While these events have succeeded in refocusing popular attention on the study of how humans learn to read and write and on the importance of language to national identity and culture, they also have further problematized the aims and methods of the English class. As a result, the category of literature is now more difficult to define, as are the goals and methods of its teaching. In the mean time, composition has risen in importance as more students come to the academy without the knowledge of how to write in academic genres and styles, and new theories have had to be developed quickly to guide writing instruction in the multi-cultural classroom.

The changes brought about by these events have primarily served to make the category of English studies less stable, and the future almost surely holds more uncertainty. But English studies seems to have been born and reared in this kind of dilemma, and the new glut of histories about English studies would indicate that these current

events are only the latest round in what appears to be an ongoing cycle
of crisis about the relationship of English studies to the culture of the
academy and to mainstream culture. Still, the latest debates do appear
often to question the very identity of English studies. The introduction
to James Berlin's *Rhetorics, Poetics, and Cultures* illustrates the
urgency with which this new dilemma is sometimes described:

> English studies is in crisis. Indeed, virtually no feature of the
> discipline can be considered beyond dispute. At issue are the
> very elements that constitute the categories of poetic and
> rhetoric, the activities involved in their production and inter-
> pretation, their relationship to each other, and their relative
> place in graduate and undergraduate work. The turmoil within
> English studies is of course encouraged by the public attention
> it now receives. Rarely has the role of English in the political
> life of the nation been so openly discussed. (xi)

While Berlin's rhetoric may be purposefully hyberbolic, it does
indicate the kind of urgency with which this newest round of crisis is
presented, and the issues currently facing English studies will almost
certainly determine how work will be done within the department in
the future. Indeed, many scholars have suggested that this crisis might
well determine if the department will exist in its present form for much
longer.

Much of this crisis mentality exists, I believe, because of the often
ambiguous and at times antagonistic relationship that workers in
English studies have had with the concept of *culture* and because of the
insidious way that the primary goals of English education often have
been made invisible by its theories and practices. This ambiguity can
be heard in conversations about the "political nature" of language
instruction, and the popularity of disciplinary histories is at least a
partial attempt to justify the idea that what we do has cultural and
political consequences.

According to most of its historical narratives, the growth of
English studies can be traced to the need for a national identity in
eighteenth century Britain, which helped to launch the study of
reading and writing in what was then the vernacular language. The
original creation of English studies is at least partially attributable,
then, to a need to normalize the language and culture of a British
population that was growing increasingly diverse. The establishment
of an approved canon of texts and the standardization of linguistic,

syntactic, and grammatical convention would help to shore up the nation/state of Britain while it also served colonial imperatives to spread the culture of the motherland to its subjects abroad. As Susan Miller notes in her history of English studies, *Textual Carnivals*, the study and teaching of the vernacular were meant to make English become for the colonized what Latin had become for the British elites: the language of law, art, philosophy and high culture. But, as Miller writes, "colonizations begin, and remain, at home," and the normalization of language conventions was as important to the establishment of a national, cultural character and identity as it was to the colonial enterprise (26). Later, in nineteenth century America, the standardization of language conventions through the teaching of reading and writing helped serve the same purpose: to normalize values under the national banner and to promote the spread of American culture and ideas within the nation and, later, abroad. From the beginning, English language instruction has been more than merely the teaching of texts, words, syntax, grammar and usage; it has been a way to inscribe, disseminate, and promote culture through the representations and values carried in texts and language conventions.

Sadly, it often seems that those who engage in the promotion of culture through marketing, popular arts, and government understand and embrace the relationship between cultural values and language more readily than do scholars and teachers in the English department. Western governments have long exhibited their belief in the ability of language to transmit culture and ideology, a fact evidenced by their continued support for programs that spread Western values and ideologies through cultural exchanges. Advertisers and those who work in Western-style marketing understand that the first rule of profit-making has always been to create or to reinforce the need for a product or a specific brand name by a careful manipulation of language and sign. Advertisers and governments seem to have no problem accepting the "political" nature of text. One only needs to look at the responses to the literacy crisis of the 1980s, manufactured or real, to realize that many on the political right have recognized and embraced the relationship between language and culture, even though their responses to this knowledge have tended to be prescriptive and reactionary ripostes to the "watering down" of cultural norms and values blamed on the "permissiveness" of the 1960s and 70s.

Meanwhile, scholars and teachers who work within English studies too often continue to struggle with humanist and aesthetic perspectives and to exhibit uncomfortable feelings about the idea that the linguistic conventions they promote and the texts their students read inscribe any values other than the aesthetic or "human" qualities promoted by what has often been called an Arnoldian perspective. Scholars and teachers have not been universally eager to accept that part of their practice is to serve and promote nationalist ideology and mainstream cultural values. Admittedly, more than a few scholars and teachers have responded to the new crises posed by diversified enrollment and postmodern/poststructuralist influences by supporting the expansion of the canon to include formerly excluded literatures, by permitting the study of certain elements of popular culture such as film and advertisement in their literature and writing classes, and by increasing their tolerance of individual, ethnic, and class difference in their writing assignments. Still, these concessions and affirmations have not been enough to promote substantial change. In fact, critics such as Stuart Hall caution that these moves do as much to institution-alize, engulf, and appropriate other cultures as they do to expand the subject and methods of English studies and to make them more relevant.

Some, such as Berlin, have argued that the best course for English studies is to focus on "reading and writing the daily experiences of culture, with culture considered in its broadest formulations" (*Rhetorics* 116). This move may serve to incorporate popular and marginalized literatures and genres into the subject of English classes, but there also are serious questions as to how much this practice actually changes. For example, Stanley Fish worries that,

> if, for example, we "forge connections to popular culture" by writing about it in addition to or in place of writing about Shakespeare and Spenser we will merely have added another room to our academic house. This will not mean that the boundaries of the profession will have been pushed outward. Bringing new grist to the mill does not in itself alter the basic manner of its operation. (101)

In fact, it often seems that scholars and teachers of English studies have not really given up their concern with sorting texts and conventions into "low" and "high" categories but have merely become fascinated with that which they used to call "popular" or "low" culture. In the English class, texts from popular culture are still often either exotic oddities or mere substitutes for canonical texts. The roots of this problem are deep, and the ambiguity toward culture and cultural value and the controversy over what constitutes literature and literacy can be seen throughout the history of English studies.

Scholars have been fond of tracing the genesis of this controversy to the eighteenth and nineteenth centuries, when the high priests of the neo-classical and Romantic eras responded with their own crisis mentality to the spread of popular culture brought about by the industrial revolution. Critics warned, as Matthew Arnold did in *Culture and Anarchy* (1867), against the spread of a "philistine culture" that would divide the culture and keep it from achieving its own greatness. Later, Eliot advised that popular culture was only to be studied in order that it might be condemned for its shortcomings and lack of aesthetic value. Conveniently, these efforts to split culture into distinct "high" and "low" categories allowed scholars and teachers, who by the late nineteenth century were establishing a firm canon and method, to isolate the subject of English studies from "mass" or "popular" culture, or at least to convince themselves that those texts and conventions they accepted were somehow better at expressing essential human experiences and beauty than were those they chose to exclude.

To a large extent, many new theories of reading and writing signal a final recognition of English studies' role in acculturating the student, but this acceptance is not without critical consequences for the discipline. One should not believe that all but the most traditional scholars accept as valid the study of how linguistic and textual representation serve power relations. Scholars such as Fish and Hall have questioned specifically the appropriateness and effectiveness of turning to theories like cultural studies, and have offered disturbing visions of an impotent English department serving up watered-down texts to a student population it considers naive innocents. Susan Miller and Bruce Robbins, among others, also have begun to problematize the link between culture and English studies in a way that argues that cultural studies and the movement to value diversity of expression within the academy might be just another way to promote and reinscribe the cultural and academic status quo.

Still, the crisis continues. Intent on protecting its place within the academy and culture, English studies has begun to examine the conditions of its birth and up-bringing in order to work its way out of the uncertainty of a middle age in which its purpose and meaning have been so radically challenged. Within the department, composition and literature labor to redefine their places, with only a sense of their shared history to create an identity strong enough to hold them together. Outwardly, the department struggles to counter the suggestions by the right that it return to a promotion of the traditional canon and the teaching of basic writing and rhetorical skills as a means of solidifying national identity and of providing students with workplace skills. In order to begin to come to terms with these difficult issues, I think an understanding of the troubled relationship between English studies and culture is necessary.

English Studies and Culture

As Raymond Williams points out, "culture is one of the two or three most complicated words in the English language" (76). In fact, the early English versions of the word were usually employed to refer to the tending of crops or animals, and only later was this action extended to the development of humans and, even later, to the cultivation of their minds. The use of the word as an independent noun indicating a broad concept akin to the word "civilization" is a relatively new occurrence. However, according to Williams, the German philosopher Herder, who as early as 1784 was already ridiculing the idea that human advancement was either linear or progressive, pointed to the possibility that imposing and promoting specific social values could be an effective means of normalizing diverse populations. Herder already recognized that values could be geographically situated or ethnically specific, and he was among the first to separate consideration of human development into "material" and "human" aspects. In this split, the word *culture* originally held fast to its roots in agronomy and was, at least until Matthew Arnold, most often used to refer to the material aspects of human social and individual development. The word *civilization* most often signified "spiritual" or "aesthetic" development. However, from the beginning the ability to control the definition of the word *culture* has been essential to those who would split human activity, thought, and endeavor into "high" and "low" categories. In a revealing passage from *Keywords*, Williams writes:

> Hostility to the word "culture" in English appears to date from
> the controversy around Arnold's views. . . . It is significant that

> virtually all the hostility . . . has been connected with uses
> involving claims to superior knowledge, . . . refinement (culchah)
> and distinctions between "high" art (culture) and popular art
> and entertainment. It thus records a real social history and a
> very difficult and confused phase of social and cultural devel-
> opment. (81-82)

From the beginning, the word *culture* has been a site of controversy, especially within English studies. Matthew Arnold solidified the conflict in a phrase that is as familiar in Western letters as any:

> [Culture is] the great help out of our present difficulties; culture
> being a pursuit of our total perfection by means of getting to
> know, on all the matters which most concern us, the best which
> has been thought and said in the world. (6)

Ironically, the critical gaze focused by those who have worked within this construction of culture seems capable at times of expanding to include almost any human endeavor, especially those that have human progress as their goal.

Despite talk of exclusion, this system is primarily concerned with taxonomic completeness, endeavoring to include as much of human production and thought within its boundaries as is possible in order to control what is valued as aesthetic and what is dismissed as mundane. "High" culture comes to signify that part of human endeavor that serves spiritual or humanist progress by its originality and singularity and is said to produce art; "low" or "popular" culture comes to signify that part of human endeavor that serves commercial or material progress by its accumulative or preservative function and is said to produce artifact. This familiar taxonomic scheme is conveniently diagramed in A. J. Geimas's "semiotic square" (1968). On one side of the diagram is culture; its zenith is epitomized by the traditional, the collective, history, folklore, material culture, and craft. Its nadir is the reproduced and the commercial, the curio, and the utilitarian. On the other side is art; its zenith is epitomized by the singular, the original, pieces of art, and connoisseurship. Its nadir is fakes, inventions, technology, ready-mades, and anti-art (Clifford 57).

As James Clifford points out, the problems of definition inherent in this scheme are readily forecasted: craft becomes art as museums collect "tribal" objects, curios become collectibles, furniture becomes art by the quality of its design, etc. (58-59). Nevertheless, following Arnold this construction conveniently fixes the terms *art* and *culture* within one system, and it is that system that has bound scholars and teachers of English in an endless cycle of ambiguity and anxiety over their subject's relation to the project to acculturate students. Also feeding this dilemma is the fact that categories and definitions inside the art-culture system are highly indeterminate and growing more so. As Clifford contends,

> the classifications and generous appropriations of Western art and culture categories are now much less stable than before. This instability appears to be linked to the growing intercon- nection of the world's populations and to the contestation since the 1950s of colonialism and Eurocentricm. (65)

In fact, instability was inherent in this system of art and culture from its beginning. For example, as viewed from within the system culture seems to yearn for the artistic, as is exhibited in ethnographic study and folk art movements; art seems always ready to devour culture. Arnold's and Eliot's constructions of the art-culture system portray art, or high culture, as always in conflict with popular, or low, culture; however, it is the inclusion of the two terms within the same system and the fluid relations between its two extreme positions that has allowed the line between art and culture to be blurred within the last half of this century. This is also what has made cultural studies acceptable to some English departments. Clifford explains that,

> the inclusive twentieth-century culture category—one that does not privilege "high" or "low" culture—is plausible only within this system, for while in principle admitting all the learned human behavior, this culture with a small *c* orders phenomena in ways that privilege the coherent, balanced, and "authentic" aspects of shared life. (62)

The seeds of English studies' ambiguous relationship with culture are evident in the way that the art-culture system constructs concepts of culture, both high and low, and in the desire of those who work within its construction to examine and to "know" humankind. In this system, all institutions and practices, and all texts, conventions, and genres— those that have been commonly included and praised as examples of high culture and those that have been commonly excluded and derided as low culture—are always subject to the taxonomic imperatives of those who work within the system, even as these conventions and genres move in and out of favor and fashion. In fact, at its best the impetus of Western academic theory as expressed in the practices of English studies might be described as a tendency to collect all cultural artifacts, high and low, and to put them in a glass case (or a multicultural reader), in order that they might be examined, judged, and wrung of their meaning. This can be seen even, and perhaps especially, in some academic applications of cultural studies. While those teachers and scholars who promote the study of popular texts, conventions, and genres see themselves as at war with Arnoldian and New Critical ideas of canon and aesthetics, they are just as often a part of the process by which Western academic conceptions of art expand to absorb exotic or popular cultures and their artifacts and by which exotic and popular cultures struggle to become accepted within Western culture by seeking legitimization within the academy.

Within English studies, the art-culture system exhibits itself in three primary attitudes toward culture, and these attitudes are represented in three basic pedagogical approaches to the teaching of writing and reading. These can be roughly divided into three positions: that which constructs English studies as the aesthetic arbiter of cultural value, that which constructs English studies as a service institution of social and academic acculturation, and that which attempts to resist both the aesthetic and the acculturative nature of English studies.

English Studies and Aestheticism

Critiques of Arnoldian thinking are abundant and familiar, and it is not my wish to simply deride the idea that the goal of teaching literary criticism and writing in English studies should be "to know the best that is known and thought in the world." In fact, when taken at face value, this seems like an admirable goal. But Arnold's pronouncement, however considered, contained the seeds of its own undoing, as many have pointed out. Although Arnold's own values were decidedly narrow, in service to his Christian-Anglo bias, he wrote that a knowledge of the best should be "irrespective of practice, politics and everything of the kind" (1396). The usual and perhaps obvious criticism is that Arnold was unable to see that his own position was political and interested, but an examination of his texts on the subject reveals, in fact, a blatant and unapologetic cultural agenda that is contrary to his desire to make judgments that are apolitical. Still, a more important criticism of Arnold may be that the art-culture system he helped solidify forced almost all human endeavor to submit to his critical, academic gaze. English studies, which within this aesthetic construction has meant primarily the study of literature, was to take the place of religion and the state, both of which Arnold thought had failed to create a national identity, and this construction is unabashedly political, interested, and seeks a material, cultural result. Terry Eagleton's analysis of these issues also begins with Arnold:

> The key figure here is Matthew Arnold, always preternaturally sensitive to the needs of his social class, and engagingly candid about being so. The urgent social need, as Arnold recognizes, is to "Hellenize" or cultivate the philistine middle class, who have proved unable to underpin their political and economic power with a suitably rich and subtle ideology. This can be done by transfusing into them something of the traditional style of the aristocracy, who as Arnold shrewdly perceives are ceasing to be the dominant class in England, but who have something of the ideological wherewithal to lend a hand to their middle-class masters. (21)

The point of examining Arnold, at least for this discussion, is to demonstrate that the art-culture system has been an ideal way to express the ambiguous position of the traditional English literary critic toward culture and to help render his own political and cultural agenda invisible. Within this system, culture becomes for the literary critic a term that subsumes both high art and popular culture and gives him the power to separate every endeavor of humankind into the sacred and the secular. Over time, the art-culture system has allowed scholars and teachers within English studies to distance their work from the material concerns of the everyday world, yet it has also made the commonplace available to them.

As such, to pretend that literary criticism and the teaching of literature are not part of the project to spread cultural value, and to use Arnold as an exemplar of this attitude, as many have done, is phony and misreads Arnold, and to act as though the teaching of aesthetic, rhetorical, and linguistic convention under this system is not an ideological endeavor is obviously fraudulent, as many have pointed out. At the same time, teaching culturally sensitive texts or texts from mass culture does not release English studies from the grip of the art-culture system. These methods are too often merely ways to expand the critic's theories and methods to subsume those new texts and conventions and to make them available for his evaluation (I purposely use the masculine pronoun).

Historically, English studies has been dominated by the study of textual reception, and only recently have theories about how texts and rhetoric are produced become important—at least those theories that attempt to move beyond romantic ideas of inspiration and imagination. However, although English studies has begun to examine how and why texts are produced, student compositions have never been considered actual "authorship," and so student writing has never held equal footing within academic conventions and traditions with those of "professional" authors. Writing classes have been primarily taught as,

> a consciously selected menu to test students' knowledge of graphic conventions, to certify their propriety, and to socialize them into good academic manners. (Miller 66)

Student texts, then, are designed primarily to serve as tests to affirm students' successful acculturation into the academy and not as objects of serious study.

I am not convinced that opening the canon and admitting new ways of reading will move English studies much beyond the traditional desire to "cultivate the philistines." However, cultural studies and other new theories of reading have turned our attention to the role of linguistic and textual convention in reinscribing cultural values and toward an examination of rhetoric and textual production. As such, the writing classroom might become the place to finally overthrow at least two ideas that we have inherited from the art-culture system. The first is the idea that students are not authors, and the second is that student texts have little value beyond that of certifying students as ready for more advanced study. But if student writing is to be valued in new ways, compositionists will first have to deal with the historical construction of the writing class as a service institution that attends the culture of the academy.

English Studies and Acculturative Service

Along with the advent of eighteenth and nineteenth century aestheticism, a great body of rhetorical theory, especially in America, moved away from Aristotelian notions that truth existed apart from rhetoric, and that language was primarily a means for communicating that truth. According to Berlin, American notions of rhetoric in the late eighteenth century began to embrace Scottish Common Sense Realism, which located reality "in two discrete realms, the spiritual and the material" (*Writing Instruction* 6). This construction made perfect sense to the nineteenth century aesthetic, in that it also could be used to split human endeavor into high and low categories, or in this case spiritual and material activities. Literary critics were eager to promote the study of literature as a quasi-spiritual activity, but they also were willing to accept responsibility for the "materiality" of rhetorical production, especially since the latter also could be translated into the study of literature. In fact, reading literature was thought to be enough both to cultivate human values and to teach students to produce good rhetoric. Adherents to this form of realism, such as Hugh Blair, theorized that students learned to write by reading literature and by mastering the mechanics of literary criticism (6). Unfortunately, as the century closed writing instruction that was not specifically concerned with poetics was stripped of its vitality. Literature was the way to acculturate students into aestheticism, and writing instruction became the way to acculturate students into the academy. The American university system

> divided the entire academic community into discrete parts. . . .
> As far as rhetoric is concerned, this meant that persuasive discourse—the appeal to the emotions and the will—was now seen to be possible only in oratory, and concern for it was thus relegated to the speech department. Discourse dealing with imagination was made the concern of the newly developed literature department. The writing course was left to attend to the understanding and reason, deprived of all but the barest emotional content. Encouraged by the business community, with the tacit approval of the science departments, composition courses became positivist in spirit and method. (Berlin, *Writing Instruction* 9)

Thus, speech and oratory claimed persuasion, literature claimed "creative" writing, and composition became primarily a service activity designed to certify that applicants to the literature sections were at least versed in the basic skills needed to construct a sentence, a paragraph, and an essay. The rhetorical concerns of scholars and teachers of literature thus turned further and further away from persuasive, expository, and prose texts in general and toward an overwhelming concern with poetry, which they considered the highest expression of aesthetic rhetoric. True to the art-culture system, literature became "high" culture within the academy, and composition became "low" culture. Writing pedagogy was charged primarily with the material concerns of preparing students for academic culture and the study of literature (Tuman 342). Under this system, the composition class rapidly became a ghetto where teachers and their charges were concerned with parsing sentences, correcting spelling errors, and perfecting handwriting techniques. Students who were assigned to take these classes were required to produce themes almost daily, and the classes most often were staffed by overworked, beginning instructors or their assistants who, for the most part, would rather have been teaching literature. A report in 1923 by Edwin M. Hopkins calculated that the work of one composition instructor at the University of Kansas, who was in charge of 105 students, would require 30 hours a week in theme reading alone (Connors 193). But scholars and teachers within English departments were certain that reading literature was enough to inspire whatever rhetorical greatness there might be in their students, once those students had proved themselves worthy of its study. The priority of the composition class became to acculturate students into the aesthetic culture of the academy, while literature would acculturate students into mainstream, Western, humanist culture.

Clearly, the events of the last forty years—particularly the rise of postmodern and post-structuralist thought, the increased enrollment of a diverse student body, and the realization of the power of language to reinscribe cultural value—have further strained the uneasy compromise that made writing instruction a part of English departments concerned almost totally with literature. Moreover, changes in the last half of this century have produced different reactions from those who work in either side of the department, often driving their interests further apart. The same revolution that encouraged departments to expand their coverage of texts from various excluded and marginalized groups and to accept new theories of reading allowed those who were concerned with teaching writing to turn composition from what was a distasteful chore for teaching assistants and hopeful literature profes- sors into a vibrant endeavor with its own growing body of knowledge and with its own respected scholars and teachers.

Now, folks in both sides of the department have begun to realize that learning to read and write academic and disciplinary texts has been primarily a way to reinforce academic and mainstream cultural value, and some have construed from that idea that writing and reading instruction could possibly be a way to implement cultural and institu- tional change. Scholars and teachers in literature have moved to redefine literature beyond its acculturative service to the nation-state, just as scholars and teachers in composition have moved to redefine the subject and methods of composition studies outside of its service to the culture of the academy and to literature. Workers in both disciplines have moved to address more directly the relationship between learning to read and write and becoming acculturated into mainstream and academic culture. Indeed, the concern now is often that students become empowered to read critically and to use writing assignments to express their own cultural and personal values. The interest in empowering students—in addition, perhaps, to "enlighten- ing" them—is certainly a first step in helping English studies break its old pattern of subsuming and categorizing that which it comes in contact with under the aesthetic system of art and culture. The second step is for English studies to reestablish itself as an institution that recognizes the work its scholars, teachers, and students do not only to reinscribe but to create cultural values.

In addition to valuing alternate readings and alternative ideas of textual production, it is theories about how student writing might be valued as authorship, how students texts might be read as literature, and how those texts directly address, contest, and express cultural value that hold the most promise for confronting the old art-culture system's taxonomy of "low" and "high" culture.

English Studies and Resistance

The acceptance of English studies' role in the reinscription of cultural values has, predictably, fostered the notion that that same power might also be used to resist acculturation or to bring about social, political, or economic change in society and in the academy. Judith Goleman writes,

> Working the theories of knowledge and systems of truth that are working them, specific intellectuals in effect redefine knowledge and truth as worldly things and, in so doing, begin to alter the systems of statements and procedures that have produced these concepts. (5)

This move builds upon the idea that language instruction is a way to transmit values and suggests that the teacher resist his or her traditional role as "universal intellectual—one, for example, who advises students on 'the regime of truth,' its systems, procedures, and effects" (5). The aspirations are to recreate the role of the teacher/critic/scholar, to resist the role of aesthetic intellectual or service worker, and to redefine the teacher as public intellectual or cultural worker. For many of these scholars and teachers, English studies seems the ideal place for dialogues that work in the spaces between art and culture, between the aesthete and the materialist, between reading and writing, between the public and the private, between the student writer and the professional author, and between the teacher and the student. These teachers see real possibilities for altering the institutions of culture and of the academy by "decentering" themselves and assuming the role of one who encourages students to question cultural and academic values, but too often their attempts have met with limited success.

The goal is questioning students.

    Sadly, the possibility that the art-culture system will again expand to subsume the theories and practices of those who would openly address the acculturative nature of English studies is very real. There is, as Berlin notes, the genuine potential that pedagogies aspiring to resist the art-culture system, "based as they are on a critique of Western idealism, are nevertheless reverting, under institutional pressure, to traditional relations with their materials and their students" ("Composition" 63). Moreover, those who hope to foster resistance to mainstream cultural values by their work in the classroom are often stymied in their attempts to control and direct the nature of those cultural changes. Berlin, for example, wants,

> students to begin to understand that language is never innocent, instead constituting a terrain of ideological battle. . . . We are thus committed to teaching writing as an inescapably political

what happens when we don't have control over language.

act, the working out of contested cultural codes that affect
every feature of our experience. (51)

But Berlin and those who have attempted to teach such liberatory
pedagogy often report a "stiff unwillingness" on the part of their
students to question and problematize the cultural values presented by
literary or other texts. Additionally, practitioners of resistance pedagogy have been roundly criticized from the right for attempting to
indoctrinate their students. At the same time, they are criticized from
the left for "failing to forward a political agenda" (52-53). While it is
easy for some scholars and teachers to come to the realization that part
of the job of the English classroom is to acculturate and normalize
students into the academy and into culture at-large, it is not easy to
know what to do with that knowledge.

Certainly, the possibility exists for some cultural change through
the teaching of reading and writing, and even though it is valuable to
recognize the importance of language in the promotion of cultural
values, it is also important to realize the small part that the English
classroom actually plays in the ordinary lives of people as they interact
with culture. Like Berlin, Evan Watkins promotes a direct confronta-
tion with culture, but also warns that English studies, "occupies a
marginal position in the larger organizing apparatuses of cultural
production and circulation with that dominant formation" (271).

Reading and Writing and Culture

In the quest to create an identity that is more than just a reaction to the
latest crisis, scholars in English studies have begun to come to terms
with the way their theories have masked the acculturative role of the
discipline. The movement to expand the canon and to develop new
theories of reading has opened the study of English to a variety of new
voices, and the acceptance of composition as an important scholarly
and teacherly pursuit has signaled that English departments are willing to consider the meaning and the methods of their acculturative
role. The questions that must be answered now, as the most vibrant and
enduring debates in our literature indicate, are questions of what we
hope to do with our students. Why do we want them to read these
particular texts? What, exactly, are we hoping they will become by
taking our classes?

The notion that we are training our students to be good humans by having them read and recreate models of the best writings of other humans is noble, but it does not question its own motives enough. The art-culture system under which most of our history has been enacted is surely a political one, as is the aesthetic humanism that it supports and that has informed the last 125 years of English studies. The English department had been changed by the expansion of the canon and by the addition of cultural studies, queer studies, gender studies, and African-American studies; but it will not be *radically* changed solely by any process of reading texts to uncover their complicity in the power structures of Western culture.

The dismal idea that we are merely training students to be good workers or good students is not satisfying enough, but neither is the idea that we must merely teach students to resist the values of the dominant culture. If the political nature of what we do is to be adequately addressed, then students must be encouraged to see themselves as authors of texts that are equal to the texts they read—perhaps not in their perfection of convention and style but in their ability to inscribe and alter those conventions and in the cultural values they represent. There is, as Bhabha writes, "somewhere between theory and political practice" a place where institutional practices, genres, and conventions become available for student authorship (18).

What is needed first is the widespread recognition that learning to write texts is at least as important as learning to read them, whether one believes that the student is being trained to become a successful manager, a responsible citizen, or a decent human being. So far, the mountain of essays that have been constructed by our students have been valued strictly for what they show about the student's readiness to attend to the more important subjects of literature and the disciplines. Student texts are, in fact, the primary texts of the composition class, and they deserve to be studied and valued for what they say about the human condition and about the necessary uses of language. Unfortunately, they seldom get much more attention than ten minutes under the red pen. These texts are a transaction between the student's position and the cultural authority of the academy, and they expose the possibility for a space of openness and availability in academic theories and practices and in mainstream culture. Students' texts are important in that they unmask the acculturative, evaluative, and taxonomic authority of traditional English studies, aestheticism, and the art-culture system.

So What Is To Be Done?

First, the push for widespread acceptance of composition as a viable content area of English studies must continue, as must the push to give sophisticated training to writing teachers. Teaching writing is unlike teaching any other body of knowledge, and it takes trained professionals to adequately address the acculturative power relations that come into play when we ask our students to write in academic genres. Writing teachers need to know how to make assignments that allow students to negotiate the spaces between themselves and the academy. Writing teachers need to be trained how to evaluate writing for more than style, logic, and surface errors; they need to know how to evaluate rhetorical situation and context and how to respond and to grade so as to encourage active engagement with the conventions and genres of the academy. In writing classes, the individual transaction with the authority of cultural, academic, and disciplinary institutions is most overt and most exposed, and it is no accident that students' most visceral reaction to academic training, either for good or for ill, is often the reaction they have to reading and writing classes. The composition classroom asks something of the students that other classes do not: it asks them to expose their inner selves and their private values in writing, and yet it most often evaluates those writings strictly as a means to assess students' readiness for "real" study or for their ability to think in what we consider a "mature" and logical way.

In practical terms, I would like to see the culture of student publications grow. Too often, student writing appears and disappears with being read by a real reader. We ask students to write essays "as if" they are to be published in the school or local paper, or "as if" they are to be collected in a larger text. Some textbook readers do include student work, but too often these works are treated merely *as* student work. Perhaps publishers should begin to collect and publish student work in a real way. So much more needs to be done to make the critical position of author available to the student.

In answer to the question "what is to be done," Bhabha answers first that "there is no knowledge—political or otherwise—outside representation" (23). Therefore, the call is to

> acknowledge the force of writing, its metaphoricity and its rhetorical discourse, as a productive matrix which defines the "social" and makes it available as an objective of and for action. (23)

Student writing is effective in countering the art-culture system of the academy not because it keeps the student and the academy separate, but precisely because academic writing and reading are agents of acculturation. The student performance of academic rhetoric in the site of acculturation creates a space where value is alienated and disjointed in the possibility of something new, and where the space between culture and the academy is revealed and occupied by the student author and his or her text.

Instead of asking students to read and write a series of static, traditional texts and modes that are meant to display the conventions of academic discourse and to prove the student's worthiness to join the culture of the academy or mainstream society, writing and reading teachers might encourage students to explore how the rhetoric of academic discourse can be made available to their more immediate needs, and this, of course, includes the need to produce texts that might be acceptable within the culture of the academy. Nevertheless, the dissonance produced as students encounter the acculturative power of the educational system provides a way to demonstrate both the power of academic discourse and its usefulness to the expression of students' values. The examination of these dissonant spaces encourages both students and teachers to see academic discourse as an incomplete and open space wherein students might inscribe their own subjectivities and their own cultural values.

The institution of English studies has always been complicitous in the project to make human production and culture subject to the academic evaluation of the literary critic and to the methods of Western critical theory. The art-culture system has allowed scholars and teachers in English studies to subsume and categorize all human activity under the master theory of culture and to render its own acculturative role invisible. Valuing student articulations as authorship and recognizing how student literature accepts and contests cultural values by hybridizing and rearticulating the conventions, genres, and forms of academic and disciplinary writing might be a way to help break the hold of the art-culture system on the teaching of reading and writing and to effectively begin to address our own acculturative role.

Chapter Two

Reproduction and Resistance

Despite the efforts of compositionists to promote writing as a critical activity, most people outside the discipline (and many within it) still think of post-secondary writing courses as skills-based remediation or as gateway classes that students must pass through to be accredited for further academic study. In particular, the first-year course is seen as a place where students should be taught to "speak the language of the academy" before they are trained by the "real" disciplines to take their places in the workforce. As Evan Watkins points out, "English in some form continues to be . . . 'universally' required because it has been marked as an avenue of access to the more economically lucrative and socially prestigious professional occupations" (6). The pathway toward stature and success may begin with composition courses, but the important work is often seen as lying beyond the gates of the composition class and through the more rigorous training of the other disciplines.

In spite of this popular conception, many compositionists have struggled to make their classrooms more than gateways. While most would agree that teaching students the standards, conventions, and genres of academic and disciplinary discourses is yet an important part of the mission of the composition class, compositionists have increasingly sought to accentuate the value of writing as an activity that can be used to contribute to and interrogate existing knowledge. In addition, many of these same scholars and teachers have taken it upon themselves to question the normative traditions of the writing class-

35

room, and one of their primary interests has been to examine how students react to the acculturative force of the classroom.

In "Conflict and Struggle: The Enemies or Preconditions of Basic Writing?" Min-Zhan Lu examines how scholars such as Patricia Bizzell, Elizabeth Flynn, Joseph Harris, Andrea Lunsford, and John Trimbur have approached the notion that "reading and writing take place at sites of political as well as linguistic conflict" (888). Generally, these scholars all have argued that students in the writing classroom engage in a transcultural conflict wherein they attempt to negotiate a crossing from their "home" cultures into the culture of the academy (888). The goal is to analyze how the acculturative mission of the academy affects student learning and student lives, and how teachers can overcome, accommodate, or employ this cultural conflict in their classroom practices.

According to Lu, these scholars make two basic assumptions about the acculturative nature of learning within the academy:

> first, that learning a new discourse has an effect on the re-forming of individual consciousness; and second, that individual consciousness is necessarily heterogeneous, contradictory, and in process. (889)

These scholars generally argue that the transcultural moment, as it presents itself in the composition class, is one of "repositioning" for the student. In the language of these scholars, students entering the academy find themselves at the "boundary" of a new culture, where they exist on the "margins" or in "conflict" with the dominant and hegemonic culture (888).

These theories about what occurs when students encounter the acculturative force of the academy are particularly interesting because they call for the space of the writing classroom to be "re-theorized," and, generally, these reconstructed writing classrooms take one of three basic shapes. In the first, the class is envisioned as a "community" of writers negotiating with each other and with the acculturative forces of the academy and society. In the second, the class becomes a "contact zone," where cultures clash and individuals reposition themselves in relation to home, mainstream, and academic cultures. In the third, the class becomes a "borderland," where individuals cross back and forth in dynamic interaction with the culture of the academy and with their own home cultures.

All of these constructions have been beneficial to critical scholars and teachers in that each suggests that the classroom can be a place where students are thought of as more than merely un-acculturated initiates. What is also useful is that each of these pedagogical theories implies the possibility of including a space to discuss what happens when students, teachers, and scholars risk non-compliant or resistant behavior to challenge the traditional acculturative and normative projects of the academy. What is most innovative about this work, though, is that scholars building upon these ideas have argued that the transcultural nature of writing instruction involves a complex dialectic wherein conflict and resistance are useful and perhaps even necessary aspects.[1] For example, Lu's article ends with a call to "find ways of foregrounding conflict and struggle," in order to highlight what happens when students resist the traditional acculturative aims of the writing class (910). This concept of *resistance* is usually taken to signify behaviors that contest the acculturative forces of the academy and that interrogate "dominant ideologies with self-aware logic and creativity" (Miraglia 416).

In this chapter, I will describe how theories about the usefulness of resistance and resistant behavior in the classroom have evolved from reproductive theories, which are theories that describe *how* dominant cultural ideologies are reproduced through the structures and practices of social and political institutions. Also, I will illustrate a few of the various ways compositionists have argued that non-compliant behaviors may be used to promote a challenge to the acculturative mission of the academy or to promote critical skills that resist the unconscious reification of dominant ideological values. Resistance theories are a useful addition to reproductive theories, I argue, in that they encourage compositionists to explore how ideological values are articulated and produced in rhetoric and discourse. However, I will suggest that this exploration should lead to a further consideration of how texts are "authorized" and distributed within the academy and the disciplines and to a reconsideration of the material and cultural work accomplished by student texts. In addition, I will argue that this reconsideration could represent the beginnings of a significant "territory shift" in how scholars and teachers of composition think about the acculturative mission of the academy and of the writing class.

Resistance and Opposition

Resistance, as it is used in this context, is a highly ambiguous and elusive concept. In pedagogical theories that consider how students respond to classroom activity, resistant behavior has most often been contrasted with behavior that is merely oppositional, although the terms *resistance* and *opposition* are often conflated or unclearly defined in the literature. Eric Miraglia examines how Henry Giroux uses the two terms:

> Giroux's terminology allows us to articulate two important and critically different categories into which compositionists have placed resistant behavior. . . . "Opposition" will denote behaviors and strategies that are regarded as resistant in a negative sense, while "resistance" will be taken to signify behaviors that are seen as resistant in a positive sense. (416)

Conversely, in much of Ira Shor's work the term *resistance* is used to denote student and teacher behaviors that work against the goals of critical pedagogy, whereas various terms such as *empowering* and *opening-up* are used to describe behaviors that work to promote critique and counteraction to dominant ideologies.

As Miraglia points out, such constructions, however they are formulated, generally present resistance theories with their first problem: binary conceptions of non-compliant behavior must be based on some evaluative method that construes one behavior as positive and one as negative. The question must then be asked: under what imperatives are the noncompliant actions and behaviors of students and teachers to be evaluated as positively resistant or as negatively oppositional? This is not a small point. The power to control what behaviors are evaluated as positive and what are negative is also the power to control and "identify behaviors as resistant (positive), oppositional (negative), or merely non-compliant (neutral)" (Miraglia 416). For now, however, I will generally accede to the evaluative methods of critical scholars such as Giroux, James Berlin, and C. H. Knoblauch, and I will stipulate that behaviors and practices that work against the unconscious reification of cultural values or that disrupt the strictly acculturative goals of the writing classroom are to be classified as *resistant behaviors*. *Oppositional behaviors* are those that merely pose a danger to the customary progression of classroom activities. This binary, which serves to separate what are "merely"

disciplinary problems from truly resistant behaviors, is clearly problematic; nevertheless, Miraglia is right in that "it is nonetheless
defensible from the perspective of the practitioner charged with
orchestrating the wide range of activities which constitute classroom
learning and teaching" (417).

Still, as Robert Brooke has shown in his now classic article,
Underlife and Writing Instruction, it is easier to decide that an activity
or behavior is resistant than it is to rule out behaviors that might at first
seem to be merely oppositional. Brooke analyzed activities such as
whispering in class, passing notes, and reading the newspaper—
activities that would appear to be oppositional within this taxonomy—
and proposed that these disruptive activities, which he calls *underlife*,
might actually be useful in that they hold the possibility of actual
productive resistance:

> it appears that the purpose of our courses is to allow students to
> substitute one kind of underlife for another. Instead of the
> naive, contained form they normally employ, we're asking
> them to take on a disruptive form. (151)

In Brooke's view, these behaviors are promising in that they are
indicative of a resistant attitude that might, if funneled into "positive"
non-compliant behaviors, lead to real resistance.

In spite of this vexing problem of definition, scholars such as
Stanley Aronowitz and Giroux, C. Mark Hurlbert and Michael Blitz,
Berlin, Harris, Knoblauch and others have proposed that resistance
theories provide a platform from which compositionists may construct
critical pedagogical approaches that contest the stasis suggested by
merely seeking to "heal" or accommodate cultural conflict in the
writing class. Since resistance theories have evolved primarily from
reproductive theories, it may be beneficial first to outline a few of the
basic tenets of reproductive theories and to examine how resistance
theories rely on and spring from their models.

Reproductive and Resistance Models of Education

Reproductive models of education are ones that generally hypothesize
that dominant cultural values are reproduced by the activities, structures, and conventions of the academy in order to support, reinforce,
and reinscribe dominant economic, cultural, or national ideologies.

Ideological reproduction in all these models is generally considered to be both unconscious and largely unintentional on the part of the people who work and who participate in these institutions. In educational institutions, ideological reproduction is seen as being embedded in everything from the physical structure of academic buildings and the placement of the desks in the classrooms to the hierarchical arrangement of the disciplines and the traditions of teacher-student relations. As they are constructed by reproductive models, schools are not, however, smoothly operating cultural factories that seamlessly acculturate passive students in a perfect imposition of dominant ideology and values. Instead, educational institutions are places where ideology is worked out in contestatory and oppositional ideological and cultural struggle.

In the *economic-reproduction* model, which relies primarily on the work of Louis Althusser, the reproduction of ideology "has a material existence in the rituals, routines, and social practices that both structure and mediate the day-to-day workings of schools" (Aronowitz and Giroux, *Education* 72). The architecture and the seating arrangements of lecture halls, the material and symbolic distribution of the administrative staff, faculty, and students all serve to reproduce the hierarchical arrangement of the dominant economic ideology. In his work, Althusser argues that ideological reproduction works through a network of determinations,

> that exercises an overseeing, or "overdetermining" control
> over social experience. The mechanism through which the
> process of overdetermination works is that of ideology.
> (Turner 25)

Importantly, the concept of ideology in reproductive models like Althusser's makes a significant break with the Marxist concept of ideology, which includes the idea of a "false consciousness." Marx argued that resistance to ideological reproduction was hindered by the individual's false sense of the self and of the self's relation to historical circumstance. Instead, Althusser argues that the self participates willingly in the reproduction of dominant ideology not because of a false consciousness but because dominant ideology is an accepted "conceptual framework" through which humans have agreed to interpret and make meaning of their experiences[2] (Turner 26).

The *cultural-reproduction* model, which is heavily indebted to the work of Pierre Bourdieu, argues that the institution of the academy works to promote the tastes and political interests of the dominant classes as necessary and natural elements of the social order:

> [Bourdieu] argues that the culture transmitted by the school is related to the various cultures that make up the wider society in that it confirms the culture of the ruling classes while simultaneously disconfirming the cultures of other groups. (Aronowitz and Giroux, *Education* 76)

Through the hierarchies of the disciplines and by teaching the linguistic and stylistic conventions of the academy, the styles and tastes of the cultural elite are naturalized and transformed into the "cultural capital" that one needs to succeed in mainstream culture.

The *hegemonic-state* reproductive model generally relies on the work of Antonio Gramsci. This model argues that dominant ideology reproduces itself through education in more abstruse and elaborate relationships among the academy, the state, the capitalist economy, and culture. This model presents a complex system of ideological reproduction that operates through a process of state dominance, which relies heavily on the concept of hegemonic discourse. In this model, the concept of hegemony signifies two things:

> first, a pedagogic and politically transformative process whereby the dominant class articulates the common elements embedded in the world views of allied groups. Second, hegemony refers to the dual use of force and ideology to reproduce societal relations between dominant classes and subordinate groups. (Aronowitz and Giroux, *Education* 83)

For Gramsci, dominant ideology is reproduced in textual representations, linguistic codes, and institutional practices. This theory includes a more historic and social perspective, "because it now takes account not just of signs and signifiers, but of their combinations in particular, culturally specific discourses" (Turner 32).

In all of these models, reproduction of dominant ideology takes place through more than simple coercion; instead, reproduction relies on a continued "structuring" of perception and a "battle for the control of consciousness" (Aronowitz and Giroux, *Education* 83). Important also is the fact that for a specific ideological value to achieve hegemony, the subject must accede to its domination by a process of naturalization in which dominant ideology is internalized as "natural" and essentially "correct."

Composition scholars have had little trouble employing reproductive theories such as those outlined above to extrapolate the possibility of resistance to the reproduction of dominant ideology in the classroom. In the effort to theorize how pedagogy might promote the demystification of hegemonic discourses and practices and encourage resistance to the reification of the values of dominant ideology, compositionists have employed reproductive models as a basis to theorize how resistance might operate and how it might be encouraged. For example, Aronowitz and Giroux write that,

> Within the last fifteen years, a number of educational studies have emerged that attempt to move beyond the important but somewhat limited theoretical gains of reproduction theory. Taking the concepts of identity conflict and resistance as starting points for their analyses, these accounts have sought to redefine the importance of mediation, power, and culture in understanding the complex relations between schools and the dominant society. (*Education* 91)

Working first from an understanding and acceptance of reproductive models, scholars such as Giroux, Shor, Berlin, and others have been active in seeking a "critical theory" of education that questions and resists the role that schools play in social acculturation:

> Accordingly, schools are analyzed as places where students are introduced to particular ways of life, where subjectivities are produced, and where needs are constructed and legitimated. . . . Central to this perspective is the need to view schools as both instructional and cultural sites. (Aronowitz and Giroux, *Postmodern* 87-88)

Critical pedagogies employing resistance theories, while struggling with ways to delineate between "positive" and "negative" noncompliance, have nevertheless offered compositionists the possibility that work in the writing classroom might be used to mount a counteraction to the acculturative and normative mission of the academy. For the critical educator, the goal is often to establish a method by which dominant ideology might be offset by classroom activities that reveal, demystify, and critique those values.

Reproductive theories have been useful, Aronowitz and Giroux argue, in that they have done much to reveal the way in which dominant cultural ideology is advanced and normalized as a part of the cultural mission of the academy; however, their critique of reproductive theories is that, by themselves, they offer no effective way to theorize a resistance to those ideological reproductions. Resistance theories, however, seek to establish a rationale and process by which students, teachers, and scholars might challenge the acculturative mission of the academy and encourage resistance to the unthinking acceptance of the values promoted by the academy (*Education* 65-133). Like reproductive theories, resistance theories propose a critique of dominant ideology, but in addition, resistance theories hope to offer "opportunities for self-reflection and struggle in the interest of social and self-emancipation" (99-100).

Aronowitz and Giroux believe that resistance theories have been under-represented in discussions of the acculturative and normative mission of the academy because

> there has been an overemphasis on how structural determinants promote economic and cultural inequality, and an underemphasis on how human agency accommodates, mediates, and resists the logic of capital and its dominating social practices. (*Education* 91)

For example, cultural studies makes use of the basic presumptions of reproductive theories to provide a rationale for critiquing the ideological representations and values found in various cultural discourses. However, pedagogical methods that provide a rationale and process for resisting those values and representations have not been widely or effectively theorized for the cultural studies classroom; nor has the usefulness or appropriateness of cultural studies to generalized writing instruction in the English department been firmly established. In fact, critiques of cultural studies are becoming more widely circulated with each passing day. Often heard among these critiques is the charge that cultural studies privileges the teacher's world view and serves primarily to endorse a particular reading of culture. Second is the charge that cultural studies infantalizes students by constructing them as naive readers who need only to be "enlightened" by the critical teacher. Third is the charge that cultural studies does little to promote genuine change in academic structures and practices.

My intention here is not to support these critiques, nor is it to defend cultural studies as it is currently practiced within the academy. Instead, my thesis is that cultural studies, like other pedagogies that focus on revealing and demystifying the values of dominant ideology, has laid some important groundwork for compositionists who wish to employ resistance theories. Cultural studies has helped force a wider acknowledgment of the acculturative nature of the writing class and has helped to turn the conversation toward a discussion of how and why texts are made.

As Aronowitz and Giroux note, resistance theories are important as an extension of reproductive theories for four primary reasons. Initially, resistance theories offer a redefinition of non-compliant behavior by proposing that such behavior does not always or merely represent errant conduct and disciplinary problems. Instead, resistance theories suggest that non-compliant behavior—on the part of the student and of the teacher—might be an expression of ethical and political indignation that issues from the revelation that academic and cultural discourses are politically motivated. Resistant behaviors also might occur as a reaction to the values those discourses promote. Secondly, like reproductive theories, resistance theories offer some hope for individuals and groups who wish to promote a critical examination of the values inherent in hegemonic discourses so that individual students and teachers might exercise a conscious choice about whether to accept or reject those values. Third, resistance theories offer a way to champion ideas of personal creativity and imagination, and they hold out the possibility that complete social normalization and conformity are not necessary or inevitable. Finally, resistance theories complexify notions of the acculturative power of education and open them up for discussion. Academic acculturation may now be viewed as a dynamic and incomplete process in which individual agency may be taken into account. Resistance, as Aronowitz and Giroux argue, "adds new depth to the notion that power is exercised on and by people within different contexts that structure interacting relations of dominance and autonomy" *(Education* 99). Resistance theories are promising to scholars and teachers such as Shor, Berlin, Harris, Knoblauch, Hurlbert and Blitz because they represent the possibility of a pedagogy that counteracts dominant ideology and the acculturative nature of the academy.

Radical and Critical Teachers

Compositionists who promote resistance as a part of their pedagogical methods have variously been labeled as promoting "liberatory," "critical," or "radical" pedagogy. These teachers have been among the most vocal within the academy in trying to work out a way to question or to disrupt the acculturative and reproductive nature of traditional writing instruction. For them, there is at least the possibility that the writing classroom could be a space where the multiple interests of students, teachers, the academy, and society are more democratically represented and where students are offered an "explicit critique of economic, political, and social arrangements" (Berlin, *Rhetoric and Ideology* 490). At issue for these teachers and scholars is the concern that, too often, students automatically accept the values of mainstream and academic culture or that they begin to view themselves as powerless to change or to affect their own individual cultural, economic, or political circumstances or the conditions of society and the academy.

Fueled by the knowledge that the academy is an acculturative institution and inspired largely by the work of South American educator Paulo Freire, scholar-teachers such as Shor, Berlin, and Knoblauch hope to engender an interdisciplinary and cultural approach to writing pedagogy that will help students "unveil" the ideological agenda of the texts and linguistic conventions they study and that will encourage them to resist self-destructive behaviors, which are seen as the result of the uncritical reification of cultural values. The goal of these classrooms is the "liberated consciousness of students" (Berlin, *Rhetoric and Ideology* 492). Accordingly, the writing classroom for these scholar-teachers becomes the ideal place to "ground the educational enterprise in a cultural and political reflectiveness, shared by teachers and students alike, that enables liberatory action in the face of oppressive social conditions" (Knoblauch 14).

The goal of liberatory, critical, and radical pedagogy has been to foster resistance by students, teachers, and administrators to the uncritical acceptance of the acculturative mission of the academy and of the classroom and to use the power of writing instruction to resist dominant cultural, economic, and political values. These scholars and teachers hope to "empower" or "enfranchise" students—especially those from groups that have been formerly marginalized or excluded from adequate representation in cultural, economic, political, and

educational institutions. The lesson in these classes is often to resist
the passive acceptance of the values and ideology promoted by the
conventions and genres of academic and disciplinary discourses by
mounting successful critiques of the cultural values they inscribe.

In the pedagogical methods suggested by resistance theories,
questions about how members of various ethnic, gender, and class
groups view and adapt to academic and mainstream culture become
important, as do examinations of how students from these groups
affect the conventions of academic and disciplinary discourses. For
example, composition scholars such as Tom Fox and Terry Dean have
examined how students from ethnic cultures position themselves in
relation to the acculturative forces of the classroom. Marilyn Cooper,
Elizabeth Flynn, and Linda Brodkey have examined how women resist
and interact with these normative forces. Shor, Rose, Linda Brodkey,
Myron Tuman, and Joseph Comprone have all looked at how students
from "lower" classes resist and accommodate the acculturative force
of the writing class. For these scholars, the writing classroom is a site
where the personal and cultural politics of students and teachers from
marginalized cultures conflict with and create resistance to the normative forces of the academy. The important moment for these scholars
is the one in which the individual's previously held "home" values
come into contact with the values of dominant culture. In this moment,
the agenda is two-fold:

> to teach students to write as critics of their culture, to reflect on
> those discourses—of the home, school, church, media, work
> neighborhood, and so on—of which they are a part. But we also
> want to talk about teaching itself as a form of cultural criticism,
> about classrooms that do not simply reproduce the values of our
> universities and cultures but that also work to resist and ques-
> tion them. (Harris and Rosen 58)

Critical compositionists are determined to make writing instruction
deal more intimately and actively with conflicts and uncertainties of
both students and teachers, and to encourage discomfort and even
"incoherence" in the writing class. This kind of pedagogy proposes
that teachers "challenge the politics and economics of the markets" in
which academic and disciplinary writing skills "are supposed to be
useful" (Hurlbert and Blitz, "Resisting" 1).

Significantly, Hurlbert and Blitz refocus their theorizing away
from cultural texts and toward activities that directly address the

[handwritten: Narrios]

acculturative power of disciplinary discourses. They propose that by forcing "incoherence—a loss of composure" into discussions of academic discourse conventions students might be encouraged to see those conventions as unstable, dynamic, and incomplete. By featuring *disciplinary* discourses as the site of demystification and resistance as opposed to *cultural* discourses, Hurlbert and Blitz hope to highlight the specific ways in which the culture of the academy reproduces and preserves itself (7). Importantly, their theorizing includes an exhortation to compositionists to examine and resist their own positions within the mechanisms that reproduce cultural values and dominant ideology. Teachers are urged to exhibit a critical participation in the administrative and professional practices that reinforce and reinscribe the cultural values of economic, cultural, and national ideologies. James Sledd agrees:

> We should begin at home, in a sustained attempt to break the prevailing system of exploitation in our own departments—the exploitation of graduate students and part-timers, the general dislike for teaching composition, the general injustice to composition teachers. (147)

For scholars such as Sledd, it is not enough to attempt to emancipate and liberate our students by demystifying and critiquing the cultural values of the disciplines and of mainstream culture. The job of the radical compositionist must also be to critique and resist the hierarchies and injustices of the department and of the academy.

Critical teachers and scholars in composition have taken the idea that the academy is an acculturative institution and proposed that ideological reproduction can and should be revealed and critiqued in the classroom and in the professional practices of compositionists. Additionally, they have argued that non-compliant behaviors by students and by teachers might be encouraged in order to raise a challenge to the unconscious reification of dominant ideological values. In fact, radical scholars and teachers have argued that the writing classroom is the ideal place to mount this critique and to foster resistance. The goal is often to create "liberated" students and teachers who might presumably use their new consciousness to alter the cultural, economic, and political institutions of the academy and of society at large.

[handwritten: You can't make people resist. How do you make that level of engagement possible?]

Problems and Promises

So far, neither reproductive theories nor resistance theories seem to have proved completely satisfactory in the pursuit of a pedagogical method that promises genuine "liberation" for students, teachers, scholars, or society in general. To be fair, the practices suggested by these theories certainly have helped change the way in which some within the academy view the acculturative role of education and the writing classroom, and many students do, in fact, respond positively to critical or radical pedagogy. Beyond that, it is debatable just how much critical scholars and teachers have affected the way the academy functions, although the status of those who teach composition may be said to have risen somewhat, as has the general understanding of the epistemological and critical uses of writing and writing instruction. Some of these improvements must be credited to an increased aware-ness of the acculturative nature of the academy and to the encourage-ment of resistant practices. A more difficult job, however, would be to show that resistance theories have demonstrably altered the structures or practices of mainstream economics, culture, or politics in any specific, provable way. Nonetheless, reproductive and resistance theories have, in fact, given composition scholars and teachers a way to discuss how the normalization and naturalization of ideological values is promoted through the structures and practices of the acad-emy, and this is an important contribution to pedagogical theory. More specifically, resistance theories have provided a way to retheorize non-compliant behavior in a way that recognizes the dialectical nature of the cultural transactions that do take place in the classroom. In addition, resistance theories have given the more optimistic and self-reflexive scholars and teachers of rhetoric and composition a rationale for examining and possibly altering their own classroom practices.

Resistance theories have, perhaps, provided hope for some im-provement in the structures and practices of the academy. At the very least, the open discussion of the acculturative nature of the academy has provided a language in which to theorize freedom from the unquestioned acceptance of dominant cultural values. This discussion also has given more optimistic scholars and teachers encouragement in the project to use their theories and practices to mount a self-reflexive, continuing critique of the part played by the academy and its scholars and teachers in reinscribing hegemonic cultural ideology.

A problem for critical pedagogy, as many radical scholars and teachers have noted, is the fact that a great many students already may have been fully acculturated into dominant culture by the time they arrive in the composition class. Knoblauch reports,

> My students accept the stories about freedom and self-actualization, fair play and altruism, progress and prosperity that their history books have composed to portray the American experience. In accepting them they are not more naive than their parents or their teachers. They believe that Abraham Lincoln and Martin Luther King together emancipated black people. . . . That equal opportunity is a liberal euphemism for reverse discrimination. . . . That the patriarchal oppression of 20, 200, and 2000 years ago . . . has given way . . . to gender equality. . . . My students have heard about oppression in other parts of the world . . . but its unfortunate existence does not serve as a call for interference elsewhere and still less as a call for self-scrutiny at home. (13)

Berlin, Knoblauch, Shor and others have reported that, too often, the resistant behaviors they see in their classrooms are ones that challenge the critical teacher's urging that students examine, critique, and resist the ideological values of academic and cultural discourses, and that student behaviors too often demonstrate a willingness and desire to accept dominant values as "the way of the world," and to resist problematizing "the ideological codes inscribed in their attitudes and behaviors" (Berlin, *Composition* 52). These problems have caused some to question the primary tenets of resistance theory, for if our students have come to our classes in order to join mainstream culture—to get a good job in the managerial class—then isn't it also our ethical duty to help them do just that? Jeff Smith argues that

> gates are being kept, whether we like it or not; these gates open up (or bar the way to) membership in what might loosely be called "the overclass": that most of those who opt for higher education share a desire to enter that class; and that they see college both as one of those gates and as a key for unlocking others. (306)

Still, this view, while deserving of attention as a warning to those teachers who push their own agendas at the expense of legitimate student concerns, is largely an uncalled-for reaction. A review of the texts of Berlin, Shor, Knoblauch and other radical scholars and teachers shows an acute awareness of the gatekeeper role they serve as teachers of composition. Berlin writes that

> English teachers are asked to perform important functions for our society, functions that operate in a manner not necessarily immediate and obvious. Regardless of our avowed intentions, by evaluating students and influencing them to be particular kinds of readers and writers, we finally perform the job of gatekeeping and consciousness formation. (*Rhetorics* 179)

The fact that these scholars are concerned with the possibility of resistance is not an indication that they have neglected or rejected their roles as gatekeepers, as Smith seems to suggest. While compositionists who advocate critical pedagogy may hope that their methods produce radical critique and resistance, they also are usually sensitive to the legitimate concern that students need to learn the conventions and the traditions of the academy. I think that this is evident in the fact that most critical scholars insist that teachers must disclose their own political agendas to the students. Still, if critical teachers are to promote real resistance, they must stress even more the decentering of classroom authority.

Highlighting a further problem for critical teachers, Watkins cautions that the acceptance of a "political praxis" represents a "peculiar trap for anyone committed to a politics of resistance" (27). Watkins points out that the critical work rehearsed in English classes is not generally practiced in the mainstream culture. Little time is available in most jobs for the kind of "cultural criticism" that is currently practiced and promoted by radical and critical pedagogy. Additionally, English education at the post-secondary level accounts for less than one year of most people's lives, and in the "real" world, work conditions are not usually conducive to self-reflexive critique and resistance. As Watkins notes, "we'll look a long time to find something somewhere else that looks like 'resistance' as we know and love it—in 'writerly' texts and trenchant analyses of semiotic codes" (28).

English studies may, in fact, be strategically placed to promote resistance to dominant ideological values as they are expressed in textual representations and linguistic or semiotic codes. However, there is little support or demand within the mainstream culture for critical activity of that sort outside of the English classroom, and the idea that genuine, lasting, and widespread resistance to dominant ideology can be mounted from the space of a politicized writing classroom may be easily dismissed at first. Still, the situation is far from hopeless for radical and critical scholars and teachers. Certainly, writing and reading teachers can take advantage of their strategic position to support whatever "positive" changes are already happening in mainstream culture, and there is still some reason to hope that working to promote resistance may have some results beyond the English classroom:

> Political praxis in English can only work to support what is politically possible as resistance as it emerges in different forms in whatever locations throughout the social formation. That is, the political values of our work are contingent on the location of work, and that location I think dictates that we function in the education of a support structure. It will mean giving up the dream of transubstantiation, of a cultural avant-garde suddenly and miraculously emerging as also a political vanguard. But for a change it might also mean that the work we do has consequences for revolutionary change. (Watkins 28-29)

Under the circumstances, the projects of critical pedagogy are still ambitious and pose several particular problems. First, a clear way to reconcile the gatekeeper role of the composition teacher with the liberatory role is difficult to outline, and the emancipatory goal of critical pedagogy and resistance theories is far from unproblematic. The reports from those such as Berlin, Shor, Knoblauch, Bizzell and others who have attempted to mount real resistance to dominant ideological values in the classroom and in the administration of English studies have not been completely promising. And, as Hurlbert and Blitz point out, the open promotion of resistance may be professionally dangerous for composition scholars and teachers:

> Writing teachers committed to encouraging critical consciousness and action are in the potentially dangerous and endangering role of teaching people to challenge an institution's "mission." This is the kind of whistle-blowing that might very well bring about economic and social hardship among those who attempt it. In other words, the commitment involved in a critical

education extends far beyond a writing or literature pedagogy and entails very real risks in public life. ("An Uncomfortable State of Mind" 43-44).

Articulation and Production

Despite these very real problems, resistance theories may hold continued promise for those scholars and teachers of composition who wish to make their practice promote a critical resistance to the inevitable reproduction of dominant ideologies. Already, some scholars and teachers who have been involved with resistance have expressed a desire to turn the focus of writing instruction even more toward a consideration of how values are articulated and authorized both within and in resistance to dominant cultural and disciplinary discourses. Watkins, Miller, Lu, and Bruce Horner have all suggested that breaking down the binary between student writer and author may help to refocus classroom activity. Critical teachers should focus even more on promoting the idea that student texts can have material results and on examining how critique and resistance in the classroom might support critique and resistance in the academy and in the general culture. Resistance theories already have helped demonstrate the fact that embedded in the dominant cultural ideology is an invalidation of the idea that the production of student texts constitutes actual authorship. This denigration of student texts is contrary to a basic conclusion that must be drawn from resistance theory: that critical consciousness and resistance can at least change the classroom. Bruce Horner writes:

> There is also the dominant's denial of the materiality of writing, which we can see operating in the binaries distinguishing art from mechanical craft and the academic from the "real," part of a chain of binaries linked to the Author/student writer and the individual/social binaries. . . . Failure to locate student work materially can interfere with the best intentions of teachers to locate student writing in the social. (506)

The move to value the materiality of student writing shifts the focus away from writing that is merely a demonstration of the student's acceptable acculturation into the academy and culture and toward the idea that writing, even student writing, has real material consequences.

As it is, the most visible product of writing classrooms now are the grades that teachers assign to students, which are then used to promote or inhibit the student's advancement within the academy. In spite of that sobering fact, scholars and teachers who have promoted critical and resistant pedagogies are beginning to suggest that students in the writing classroom have the potential to engage in the real production of cultural texts instead of merely writing documents that certify their readiness for academic work or that demonstrate their effectiveness at mounting standard classroom critiques. Even though student texts might not currently circulate much beyond the space of the classroom, they do represent the possibility that everyone involved in the class may engage in real cultural work. As scholars and teachers of composition, we have the opportunity to focus our attention on teaching students that the production of writing is valuable work inside and outside the academy, and to concentrate on teaching critique and resistance of the acculturative roles of both student and teacher by promoting critical and resistant writing as a genuine social and material practice.

The Future for Resistance

Watkins reminds us that "what our position in the English department affords us is the chance to educate a support structure for resistances elsewhere" (272). In order to accomplish this,

> alliances must be forged . . . in terms that recognize where cultural work involves continually contested zones existing along the boundary points of contact, the movement of a population through the educational system. (255)

Clearly, the future of pedagogical methods that hope to challenge the traditional acculturative nature of the writing class lies in the movement to resist the barriers that keep student writing from having real authority in the class, in the academy, and in national culture. However, if student writing is to have real material effects, both in the lives of the students and in academic or national culture, then compositionists must develop strategies to expose, critique, and resist the way academic culture constructs textual authority. Composition does, in fact, occupy a strategic site within the academy for the empowerment of students, for it is the one place where student texts may be foregrounded as actual work. In order to increase the authority of that work, we need to find ways to help each student further historicize his or her place within the acculturative moment of the writing class in order to emphasize the dialectical, the conflicting, and the social. Efforts must be made to encourage students to see their individual, personal writing as located within the clash of cultures that inform not just the composition class, but within culture itself. As Bruce Horner writes,

> In such courses, the "personal" is taken not as the discrete residence of the individual immune to the play of the social nor as yet another passive register of the social, but as a site of and for contesting meanings, building on, responding to, and revising those meanings. Newly emergent meanings of both the self and society arise in and through that process of contestation. (325)

Writing, especially student writing, must be seen as real work, "work that matters in material and social, and not just in 'personal' ways" (Horner 526). Resistance to the student writer/author binary may be promoted if ways are found to promote student texts as authoritative sites of material and social practice. Morris Young writes that

> Too often the classroom has been constructed as a site for reproduction: students are trained in standard academic discourses; they deploy these discourses as part of required practice; they become participants in a community, often reproducing the practices of that community. (52)

I would add that the culture of the academy has too often expanded to contain the activity of resistance. Merely allowing the use of popular texts and encouraging more "personal" essays is not enough.

Far from rejecting the teaching of basic knowledge and skills, critical teaching "is a recognition of the very existence of the students and the way in which they already construct themselves, construct culture, and place themselves within culture" (Young 53). The teacher's new role is indeed to resist the comfortable traditions of the writing classroom as a place where students are initiated into the academy. Moreover, the teacher must also resist making the critique and resistance of dominant values and ideology into a game that the student can master to earn a different kind of academic approval. Critique and resistance are admirable goals for the writing class, but to that must be added the goal of making students aware that they are already active participants in the creation of cultural values and in the making of social meaning and to encourage them to see the very real relationship between rhetorical production and the material conditions of their own lives. Young writes that for students

> to participate in public life and to use public language is not to lose part of themselves. Instead they theorize their roles as writers and their place in the Nation because they recognize that they are cultural workers and already live literate lives. (70)

Critical teaching is a way to resist dominant paradigms that have constructed our students as naive initiates and to move toward a more democratic and complex understanding of textual authority.

effects of political majority
- try to make me resist
rep ub/Demo values?
- teacher poli agenda -
- student disengagement
- limited to classroom effect.
- no teacher promotion?
- resisting the teacher?
- resisting resistance?

Chapter Three

Ethics and the Writing Class

At its most basic level, the idea that writing instructors are engaged in a political activity has been hard to resist. As teachers point out that some discourse conventions are favored over others, the question seems obvious: what processes establish those favored conventions? This is, at its heart, a political question, for the power to control what conventions are "correct" is also the power to exclude those who cannot or do not wish to master those conventions. As Patricia Bizzell has written, merely "to point out that discourse conventions exist would be to politicize the classroom" (Bizzell 99).

While there is no clear consensus on what people mean when they refer to the "politicized classroom," more and more teachers have at least felt obligated to consider what political forces influence their pedagogical choices. If teachers consider how writing pedagogy has been used to reinscribe conventional discursive values, then they must also consider how those same conventions reinforce and promote cultural values. If writing pedagogy can be used to promote cultural values, then it can also be used to encourage resistance to those values.

For many, the realization that the academy has too often been a site of reproduction for elitist and exclusionary ideologies has led them to consider that classroom activities might be fashioned in a way that resists exclusion. For scholars who are concerned with extending the power of the academic experience to marginalized and formerly excluded groups, it is not too hard to see the political prospects of opening up academic, disciplinary, and cultural rhetoric to the plural-

57

ity of these voices. In fact, new knowledge about the ideological power of language has led some critical teachers to consider the tempting possibility that real political changes might result from writing pedagogy, especially pedagogy that teaches students to resist the passive reification of cultural values. However, as soon as rhetoric and discourse are presented as always persuasive and always ideologically interested, questions naturally arise about whose values are being promoted in the classroom and about how much students profit and lose by accepting or resisting those values.

In the writing class, the goals and methods of the teacher always serve some political end, whether the teacher chooses to approach writing instruction as a project to teach students the skills necessary to "speak the language of the academy," to become good citizens, and to succeed in their chosen professions; or whether the teacher hopes to encourage critical literacy, democratic and economic justice for society, and the liberated consciousness of the individual. Undeniably, any one or combination of these goals proposes an outcome with very real material and political consequences for all the parties involved. As such, teachers face crucial ethical decisions about what goals and imperatives are to inform and guide their choices and about which of these interests—those of the students, the academy, or of the state—they best serve.

In this chapter, I hope to reinforce the idea that "politicized" writing pedagogy can benefit greatly from an engagement with the postmodern perspective, especially the postmodern notion of ethics. From the postmodern perspective, reading and writing are activities that require authors and readers to make compelling political *and* ethical choices, and this chapter will examine how the thread of post-structuralist theory has tied the postmodern notion of ethics specifically to a critique of the politics of discourse and to the specific acts of reading and writing.[1] In order to engage the notion of postmodern ethics, I am also compelled to argue against the still-popular idea that ethics under a postmodern perspective must be situational, relative, and hyper-individualistic. In fact, I hope to reinforce two major ideas: that the postmodern perspective is one that is very much concerned with questions of values and ethics, and that the link between postmodern ethics and rhetoric makes the subject of ethics crucial for the writing classroom and for scholarly research by compositionists.

The idea that compositionists must be concerned especially with examining, revealing, and teaching how political and ethical values are expressed in rhetoric is supported by the fact that the writing classroom is the place within the academy where student, teacher, and institutional values most often meet in rhetorical exchange. Generally, no other class in the university asks its participants to expose and examine their own values in quite the same way that writing classes do.

Ethics, Rhetoric, and Politics

Pedagogies that include an active questioning of how ideological values are promoted by various discourses and that hope to teach how rhetoric may be employed to reinscribe or to resist ideological values are, by definition, concerned with the political and the ethical aspects of writing. As James Porter points out, the production of rhetoric is always bound up with questions of ethics and politics:

> [Ethics, rhetoric, and politics] are tied together by virtue of their common aim. The three arts can be seen to have a mutually reinforcing function: Ethics is the practical art of determining the social (as well as personal) good; politics is the practical art of implementing the social good; rhetoric is the productive art enabling ethical and political action. (210)

While the close relationship between ethics and rhetoric in Western thought can be traced back as far as Aristotle, specific aspects of the postmodern perspective can be said to promote a renewed and heightened interest in the linking of ethical and political concerns with the production and reception of rhetoric. As Porter notes, the postmodern perspective first challenges instrumentalist views of language and rhetoric and then argues against a "dialectic that can proceed unaffected by rhetorical constraint like audience and situation, a dialectic based on truth and fact, no opinion" (211).

Generally, the postmodern perspective has shifted the way many scholars think about discourse and rhetoric and about the relationship of language to ontology and epistemology. Specifically, the postmodern perspective denies the transparency of language and the logocentric idea of the autonomous author, and, as Neville Wakefield writes, postulates that the field of "meaning has been dispersed or redeployed across a much larger site of struggle and contestation" (21). If one accepts a constructionist view of language in place of an instrumentalist one, as the postmodern perspective would seem to require, then one can never again take for granted that rhetorical choices are merely stylistic variations used to elaborate ideas that exist in the mind of the author prior to or apart from language. Instead, a constructionist view of language argues that rhetoric and discourse work to build meaning within a social and historical context from which the author and reader cannot be separated. In addition, the postmodern perspective generally argues for a more intersubjective construction of what constitutes authorship and readership—a construction that I will discuss later in this chapter.

As historically situated institutional functionaries, and as the primary "authors" and "readers" of our classroom pedagogy, we can no longer pretend that the conventions we promote by our pedagogical preferences and the ways in which we evaluate classroom activities are politically or ethically neutral or that they exist apart from the ideological formulations that overdetermine our own personal and political positions. The traditions of cultural and academic discourse that we teach are not merely empty structures waiting to be filled with meaning, as the traditions of genre, word choice, syntax, and rhetorical arrangement are not merely tools that exist apart from ideas. But believing that these conventions are politically loaded requires a new way of thinking. As Terry Eagleton writes, "we have shifted from thinking of words in terms of concepts to thinking of concepts in terms of words" (*Discourse* 193). In other terms, we have become concerned with examining why certain traditions have come to dominate academic and cultural discourses.

As the conventions and genres of various discourses are no longer seen as neutral elements of style, so texts are no longer viewed as items written by autonomous authors and read by autonomous readers whose activities in these situations can be separated from the materiality and historicity in which they live out their daily lives. Rhetorical production and reception and their instruction in the academy must be viewed as occurring in a politically and ethically charged site, where the various interests of the nation and mainstream culture contend for expression, and where the ethical and moral values of students and teachers are constantly challenged or reinforced.

As composition has struggled to gain disciplinary status, it has looked to language theorists to explain how discursive systems work. The increasing awareness among compositionists of the work of structuralist and post-structuralist theorists such as Voloshinov,

Pêcheaux, Bahktin, Vygotsky, and Saussure has reinforced the project of critical teachers to encourage a deeper understanding of how syntactic, grammatical, semiotic and lexical structures serve to promote and construct ideological values.[2] The work of these theorists has helped promote the general idea that discursive processes are inscribed within the ideological relations of the public and personal situations in which they are produced and in which they are received. Critical scholars in English studies have taken these ideas and used them to promote an analysis of how language and text are bound up in the context and contingency of the material and historical situations from which they issue. More importantly, the enterprise of critical teachers has been expanded to encourage an active critique and resistance to the reification of ideological values as they are reinscribed through the rhetoric of various academic, disciplinary, and cultural discourses.

Undergirding critical pedagogy is the idea that writers can be made more consciously aware of what overdetermining ideologies permeate the linguistic and lexical conventions and genres they employ and what ethical and political positions inform their roles as authors. Also important to critical pedagogy is the idea that readers can be taught to be more attuned to the full complexity and possibility of meaning in the texts they read and to recognize the reader's role in the construction of textual meaning. Informing some of the activities of critical pedagogy is the idea that the specifics of how each discursive act is "fixed" in relation to ideological formations is often concealed both from the author and from the reader by a process in which values are internalized and naturalized, and so it is supposed that the more complex "meaning" of language can be made increasingly apparent by careful critique that includes attention to the situations in which the text is produced and received. Pêcheaux calls this process by which ideological values are concealed "forgetting." In an examination of this idea, Eagleton explains that the author or reader typically

> "forgets" the discursive formation which sets him in place, so for this mode of thought ideological representation involves repressing the *work* of language, the material process of signifying production which underlies these coherent meanings and can always potentially subvert them. (*Discourse* 197)

This process of "forgetting" is at least part of the exigency fueling the move in composition toward critical pedagogy and resistance theory. However, this idea should not suggest that critical teachers generally teach that rhetorical production must be duplicitous or manipulative to be effective or that critical pedagogy assumes that student writers and readers come to the classroom completely naive and ignorant of the persuasive nature of rhetoric. My own experience is that many students are often already somewhat adept at reading texts—at least cultural texts—when they come into the classroom.[3] Instead, the project of most critical teachers is to encourage students to *develop* their critical sense of how ideological values become associated with the production and reception of specific texts or with particular discourse conventions and to encourage them to be more aware that disciplinary and academic discourses also are motivated and informed by particular ideological formations. More important for the writing class, critical pedagogy encourages students to consider seriously the possibilities and potentials of the role of author and to examine the ethical responsibilities of writing and reading.

The emphasis on the concealed nature of ideology is not intended to construct the beginning writer or reader as a naive innocent who must be initiated into the analytic secrets of critical writing and reading skills. Teaching that rhetoric and discourse are political and ethically interested is much different from expounding the elitist idea that "ordinary" people live naively behind a veil of ignorance that hides their enslavement to ideological mechanisms and that this veil must be lifted by the application of an exclusive academic analytic before the uninitiated will finally see the "reality" of their situations. Instead, critical pedagogy only encourages a strategic awareness of the ideological nature of all rhetoric and discourse and sponsors the right of the individual or group to resist or accept the values promoted within those conventions. Above all, critical pedagogy that is informed by the postmodern perspective is concerned with making the role of author available to students and with increasing the awareness of the ethical obligations and possibilities of rhetoric and textual production and reception and the teaching of those activities.

Additionally, it is important to point out that the project to increase general awareness that discourse and rhetoric are ideologically loaded is not necessarily indicative of an irrational or over-riding fear of state or cultural institutions; nor does it necessarily promote rampant individualism—two charges that have been leveled specifically at critical and resistance theories in composition. Instead, as Eagleton writes, the project of postmodern critical theory is primarily to encourage an awareness that rhetorical production can be

> arrested into "closure"—into the sealed world of ideological stability . . . constricting the free play of signifier to a spuriously determinate meaning which can then be received by the subject as natural and inevitable. (*Discourse* 197)

The opportunity for closure described by Eagleton is a "provisional effect of any semiosis whatsoever" (197), and critical literacy promotes as its ethic an awareness and critique of how discursive closure operates to naturalize and internalize dominant values. Additionally, critical pedagogy proposes resistance to the finality of this closure by making the discursive space an available site of productive work for students to address those values in their own texts. As Eagleton notes, an awareness of the relationship between ideology and linguistic codes may be "politically enabling rather than constraining" (197). Encouraging students to be more aware of the interestedness of discourse and urging them to see discursive space as an available and productive site for their own voices promotes an empowering of the student position. Moreover, teaching students that discourse is political requires concomitant instruction in the ethics and responsibility of the positions of reader and writer.

Still, if compositionists accept the premise that every discursive utterance and convention is always persuasive of some ideological value and that meaning is forever contingent on the materiality of rhetorical production and reception, then those involved in the teaching of language also face compelling and fundamental questions about how their own political and ethical values inform their teaching and about the role they play in promoting the specific ideological and ethical values contained in the textual and linguistic conventions they teach. If rhetoric and rhetorical instruction must always be ideologically motivated, then it becomes necessary for scholars and teachers of composition to examine the material, political and ethical possibilities and motivations of their own pedagogical methods and of the discourse conventions they promote. — what is the difference b/t recognizing + Not?

Ethics and the Postmodern Perspective

The word *ethics* has been used traditionally to refer to various foundational systems of assessment and evaluation used to define and prescribe actions and behaviors in terms of right and wrong or good and bad. These evaluative terms, which are not always easy to define consistently even in the most foundational of systems, have been made even more untenable by the postmodern perspective. If nothing else, the postmodern perspective problematizes the idea that evaluation can be grounded in axiomatic or foundational systems that provide a consistent model for action in every situation and from every perspective. Specific axiomatic systems for determining the rightness of actions and behaviors based on an inherent understanding of human rights or on logical reasoning are no longer seen as reliable or always applicable across the globe, the nation, or even within the classroom. In fact, the postmodern perspective suggests that the search for a final ecumenical truth founded in nature, religion, or rationality is all but futile. Zygmunt Bauman writes that

> the foolproof—universal and unshakably founded—ethical code will never be found; having singed our fingers once too often, we know now what we did not know then, when we embarked on this journey of exploration: that a non-aporetic, non-ambivalent morality, an ethics that is universal and "objectively founded," is a practical impossibility; perhaps also an oxymoron, a contradiction in terms. (10)

The postmodern perspective argues that the project to find an infallible means for evaluating every action and behavior within the infinite multiplicity of perspectives and situations is finally impossible; nevertheless, it would be a mistake to believe that the consideration of ethics is therefore irrelevant within the postmodern perspective. Instead, the unavailability of foundational systems in which humans may ground every action and every behavior makes the study of ethics even more crucial to those who choose to adopt a postmodern perspective.

In place of rigid codes for choosing and evaluating actions and behaviors, some scholars and writers have advanced the idea that ethics is more useful as an action of open-ended critique. One version of this move away from axiomatic and foundational systems and toward a more critical conception of ethics is defined by Porter:

> Ethics in the postmodern sense, then, does not refer to a static body of foundational principles, laws and procedures; it is not to be confused with particular codes or with particular sets of statements about what is appropriate or inappropriate behavior or practice. Ethics is not a set of answers but a mode of questioning and a manner of positioning. That questioning certainly involves principles—but it always involves mediating between competing principles and judging those principles in light of particular circumstances. Ethics is decision making—but it is decision making that involves question and critique. It is informed, critical, and pluralistic decision-making. (218)

Unfortunately, Porter's view of a vital postmodern ethics in which values are determined by mediation and where pluralist critique governs decision-making is not the popular understanding of what the postmodern perspective means for ethical evaluation. More often, the postmodern perspective has been celebrated or feared as one in which all the lines that have tethered humanity to its governing institutions and concepts have been loosed and in which chaos and relativism reign. In one view of the postmodern perspective, ethics and morality no longer have any usefulness, and hyper-individualism is the rule. According to this interpretation, people who embrace the postmodern perspective are no longer willing to defend and pursue moral decency, ethical action, or political and social justice and instead base their actions and behaviors on self-interestedness or on situational ethics.

Outside of the academy, these anxieties over the postmodern are often yoked to fears of academic elitism—that the postmodern perspective signals the triumph of relativism and elitist and hyper-liberal intellectualism. Within the academy, apprehensions about the postmodern perspective often are accompanied by doubts about the value of theory in general. Sidney I. Dobrin writes,

> Because anti-foundationalist theory shakes the very ground of the Western tradition and thereby seems, at least as first, counterintuitive, it should be no surprise that it frightens people; we have all invested much in the myths of "progress" and truth building, and now they are slipping away. It becomes easier to argue that such theoretical lines do not serve any positive goal

and are, in fact, counterproductive to established ways of
thinking than it is to engage these theories in more productive
ways. (*Constructing* 13)

Bauman has argued that postmodernity did not succeed modernity
as much as it resulted from the fact that the modern age reached the
stage of its own dismantling—that the ethical and moral systems of
humanism and metaphysics failed to offer final answers to the moral
questions of the twentieth century. Modernist views of ethics, he
argues, were also largely incapable of self-critical reflection. The
discursive mechanisms by which foundational systems of ethics and
morality reproduced the ideologies contained in the "metanarratives"
of religion, humanism, and naturalism were, in fact, enveloped in a
"veil of illusions" (3). The postmodern perspective, then, is the critical
moment of self-reflection when modernity recognizes its ethical
pretense in a moment of self-reflexive critique. According to Bauman,
this critical moment does not reject ethics and morality as such but
recognizes that "certain pretenses" were false and that "certain objectives" were neither obtainable nor advantageous:

> I suggest that the novelty of the postmodern approach to ethics
> consists first and foremost not in the abandoning of character-
> istically modern moral concerns, but in the rejection of the
> typically modern ways of going about its moral problems (that
> is, responding to moral challenges with coercive normative
> regulation in political practice, and the philosophical search for
> absolutes, universals and foundations in theory). The great
> issues of ethics—like human rights, social justice, balance
> between peaceful cooperation and personal self-assertion, syn-
> chronization of individual conduct and collective welfare—
> have lost nothing of their topicality. They only need to be seen,
> and dealt with, in a novel way. (3-4)

Lyotard has defined postmodernism as an "incredulity toward
metanarratives" (*Postmodern* xxiv), and, working from this idea, Julia
Kristeva has argued for a critical ethics that exists outside of the
metanarratives of religion, humanism, and naturalism. Kristeva's
construction of a postmodern ethics, which she contains in the term
herethique (her-ethics, heretic's ethics, heretical ethics), focuses, like
Porter's, on the idea of ethics as a mode of constant critical questioning that resists all globalizing and universalizing impulses: "For
Kristeva, ethics is a (political) process through which to explore both

singularities and the relations between them" (Edelstein 199). Kristeva's perspective on ethics is fundamentally social and profoundly political and seeks to operate as a process of critique:

> Ethics used to be a coercive, customary manner of ensuring the cohesiveness of a particular group through the repetition of code—a more or less accepted apologue. Now, however, the issue of ethics crops up wherever a code (mores, social contract) must be shattered in order to give way to the free play of negativity, need, desire, pleasure, and *jouissance*, before being put together again, although temporarily and with full "knowledge" of what is involved. (23)

In short, the postmodern ethic is, at least as Bauman, Kristeva, and Lyotard construct it, a discursive action of critique which resists the closure of linguistic conventions into unified and static meaning. Bauman, Kristeva, and Lyotard, like Porter, link the idea of a postmodern ethics to the action of constant discursive critique.

Pedagogy informed by the postmodern perspective would seem to demand, then, that compositionists abandon instrumentalist views of language and promote the critical questioning of how discourse conventions and genres reinforce institutional, cultural, and individual power relations. Additionally, it would seem that teachers and scholars of critical pedagogy should seek to examine how those ideological values are resisted or accepted by individuals and groups of individuals and the ethical questions these activities raise. Still, as Sandra Stotsky writes, questions of ethics and ethical evaluation seem to be largely absent from composition scholarship:

> Indeed, as scholars, researchers, and teachers in a variety of academic settings, we implicitly engage among ourselves in principled thinking and look for the evidence of it whenever we critique our own writing or evaluate our students' writings as an indication of their thinking and learning. Thus, it is surprising how little attention we have paid as composition scholars, researchers, and teachers in particular to exploring the ethical dimensions of the intellectual processes that shape what we and our students learn through our academic writing. (47)

Postmodern theorists have been particularly interested in how the production and reception of rhetoric is imbricated in the consideration of ethics and in the power structures that are active as those values are accepted or resisted by authors and readers; therefore, it does seem natural for composition scholars to be interested in the application of the view that ethical activity may now be constructed as critical activity and that such critical activity is paradigmatically expressed in the situations of writing and reading.

In fact, scholars within composition studies such as Porter, Bizzell, Berlin, Stotsky, and Gary Olson have written that ethics is a most appropriate area of research for compositionists. Olson argues that compositionists' current interest in how ideological values manifest in discursive practices across the various subjectivities of race, gender, ethnicity, and class already implicates composition pedagogy in the project to develop ethics as a critical activity:

> The current trend in composition studies to introduce into the class discussion of and writing about issues of gender, race, or "contact zones" is a supremely ethical move, in that such focuses foreground interaction with an Other. That is, contemporary composition theory and pedagogy are increasingly more concerned with ethical questions, regardless of whether ethics as a concept is introduced directly into the discussion. ("Encountering" 46)

As with Bauman and Kristeva, Porter, Stotsky, and Olson all see the postmodern ethical situation as the one in which actions over and against an Other are chosen. In the widening plurality of the "mutually autonomous contexts" available to individuals, choice and responsibility to the Other becomes paramount (Bauman 4-5). As Olson writes, the ethical situation is now viewed as "the encounter with the Other" (46). Our actions and behaviors must now be evaluated within the processes of "negotiating and renegotiating our interactions" among the inequalities and imbalances of power relations:

> Absent external, preestablished rules of ethics, how we effect this balance of needs, desires, and obligations, *how* we negotiate our encounter with the Other, is a weighty responsibility. Thus, far from being dead, ethics is perhaps more alive than ever, for now we must *actively participate* in our own moral decision making, no longer abdicating our responsibility to external forces. ("Encountering" 46)

Instead of making ethics a dead issue, the postmodern perspective makes ethics even more crucial. Postmodernity postulates a space for ethics beyond the notion that revealed or reasoned truth can be set forth by an autonomous subject or by any foundational system. Instead, ethics within the postmodern perspective comes to refer to the choices individuals make in the critical, dynamic interplay between author and reader in the intersubjective and intertextual arena of discourse.

Postmodern Ethics and Writing

Dawne McCance views the somewhat popular idea that the postmodern perspective is "ethically bankrupt" as an essential misreading of writers such as Jacques Derrida, Lyotard, Kristeva, and Michel Foucault, all scholars whose work has been essential to the development of the postmodern perspective.[4] Of special interest to compositionists is McCance's attempt to rescue the postmodern perspective from the charges of relativism and hyper-individualism and how her analysis of these major figures, particularly Derrida and Lyotard, reveals the importance of the writing situation to the postmodern consideration of ethics.

For instance, in her discussion of Derrida and deconstruction, McCance points out that one of the primary projects of deconstruction is to disrupt the idea that a text is produced from the position of one autonomous author who is in complete control of the absolute meaning of his or her text. This move shifts the focus of theories about writing away from a concern with the individual author and his or her text to a concern with the intertextuality and intersubjectivity of meaning within discursive systems. In what Derrida has called the "apocalyptic" scene of writing, the author, the reader, and meaning are all forever deferred in the multitude of voices that endlessly reconstruct meaning within a particular discourse.

Derrida considers that writing, "though it may be intended to represent, to make present, always entails absence and lack" and so the possibility of meaning is never finally closed (McCance 33). From the deconstructive perspective, the writing of a text merely engenders more writing; it does not "settle" anything. Thus, McCance construes that the ethical imperative in deconstruction is, in fact, to resist evaluating discourse only in light of the consideration of an "authorial self," and of that self's control of meaning. Instead, the deconstructive imperative seeks always to defer the finality of meaning into the dynamic and never-ending play of discursive activity.

Deconstruction shifts the concern of writing and reading away from the search for the "truth" of the text in its production or its interpretation toward a consideration of how both author and reader are constituted by the texts that inform their own writing and reading situations. The ethical imperative from the deconstructive view, then, is to answer that "which proceeds and calls every reader and writer"— namely, "the call to write" (40). This emphasis on the ethical nature of discourse points to deconstruction's concern with the ethical responsibility of writers and readers in discursive situations. As McCance writes, "we are answerable to an other that leaves its trace in a text" (40).

As in deconstruction, values in postmodern critical theory are worked out in the never-ending discursive dialogue of historically and ideologically situated writers and readers and are constantly reassessed and deferred in the intertextuality of discourse. Meaning forever resists consolidation and incorporation into the illusionary metanarrative of any durable ideological unity. The idea is that writers can resist ideologically "fixity" by a critical awareness of the essentially intertextual, intersubjective, and constructed nature of discourse. This is what makes the scene of writing so important to the postmodern perspective.

In fact, deconstruction calls for a critical awareness that resists modernity's construction of the author:

> The solitude that often accompanies the act of writing seduces writers into believing that they are engaged in individual acts of creation; it is easy to forget, while writing, that one's language belongs to a community of speakers and writers, that one has begun writing in order to reach (absent) readers, and that one's "innovative ideas" have long textual histories behind them, histories which contain many voices. (Crowley 35)

According to Derrida, as the author writes, the situation of writing requires his absence as its essential provision, while at the same time it stipulates an Other. In its consideration of the ethics of reading and writing, deconstruction, in fact, resists the charge that the postmodern perspective is ethically bankrupt and that this lack can be traced to

Derrida's idea of deconstruction. In deconstruction, the text is a public space that never reaches a totality or finality, in which meaning is possessed in essential ways neither by the writer nor by the reader. Instead, texts and discourse are ideological arenas where values are continually worked out intertextually in a ceaseless encounter with the Other whose trace is in the texts we read and who we construct in the texts we write.

Of special interest to compositionists concerned with bringing a discussion of ethical values to their writing classes is the public, dynamic, and unendingly critical nature of writing and reading under deconstruction and within the postmodern perspective. Derrida explains:

> Deconstruction doesn't supply a new model. But once you have analyzed and questioned and destabilized the authority of the old models, you have to invent each time new forms according to the situations, the pragmatic conditions of the situation, the audience, your own purpose, your motivation to invent new forms. . . . So we have to study the models and the history of the models and then try not to subvert them for the sake of destroying them but to change the models and invent new ways of writing—not as a formal challenge, but for ethical, political reasons. (Olson, "Jacques Derrida" 129)

Derrida's comments suggest that the relationship of deconstruction to critical pedagogy in composition is strong. Both are concerned with the application of writing to a critique of institutional authority as it is expressed in discourse. Both are concerned "not only with content and concepts, but with the authority of institutions, with the models of institutions, with the hard structures of institutions" (128).

Compositionists such as Sharon Crowley have proposed that pedagogical methods informed by deconstruction would work to expose the deception behind the traditional insistence "that our students compose balanced, coherent, and organized pieces of discourse" as autonomous authors working within the rigid genres of academic and disciplinary discourses (44). Instead, a deconstructive writing pedagogy would be concerned primarily with engaging students in the production of discourse that works to address the political and ethical issues that directly concern them "and would direct the resulting discourses into the communities where such things matter" (38).

Deconstruction does not offer us a new system of ethics. To do so would be antithetical to the postmodern critique of foundational ethics and of modernity's search for foundational systems or "metanarratives" to prescribe behavior and actions. Deconstruction reinforces the idea that there *can* be a postmodern ethics and that a postmodern notion of ethics is one that resists unity, systemization, and absolutes and promotes in their place a critique of discourse and discursive authority. Deconstruction supports a rhetorical perspective of ethics that embraces dynamic, constant, intersubjective, intertextual critique.

In a more direct way than Derrida, Lyotard addresses how values are constructed and worked out in the relation between the self and the Other in the writing situation. The postmodern situation of writing, for Lyotard, begins *after* the modernist metanarratives of ethics and justice. In his reading,

> these master narratives are exclusionary systems, in the first place because they are organized around a sender-addressor and closed off from the heterogeneity of the addressee. . . . This assumption of the autonomous addressor relegates justice to the sphere of cognition, where writing is denotive exhibition, and where the addressor's autonomy is taken to guarantee the referentiality ("truth") of his or her presentations. (McCance 50)

Postmodern ethics under Lyotard is constructed as critique and resistance to the autonomous, self-actualized author and the pre-written, "imposed" construction of the reader. For example, Lyotard argues for an ethics that is critically aware of the ways that one is "spoken to" before one "speaks" and that privileges "the pole of the addressee, as the only site in which the social body can hold" (*Just Gaming* 37). Lyotard describes writing in terms that emphasize the ethical interaction between writer and reader:

> Instead of being the description of an experience, conducted by an I in quest of self-knowledge . . . writing is the testimony of a fracture, of the opening onto the other. (*Differend* 113)

Ethical responsibility, for Lyotard, is not demonstrated in the cognitive understanding of good and bad that is revealed by or derived from an absolute system and certified by the authority of the text. Instead, the ethical position is considered each time we write "because we are liable for the other" (112).

Of particular interest for those concerned with the application of the postmodern notion of critical ethics to critical writing pedagogy is Lyotard's linking of writing to resistance. For Lyotard, writing from the postmodern critical perspective would *resist* the closure of meaning in the text and the construction of the position of author as one who imposes a preconceived "truth" on a self-constructed reader:

> Writing is the capacity to resist the network of exchanges in which cultural objects are commodities, and maybe to write is precisely to avoid making a book (or even a small paper or article) a commodity, but rather to oppose, to resist the simple and naive exchangeability of things in our world. (Olson, "Resisting" 173)

A writing pedagogy based on the postmodern critical perspective would resist the closure of discourse into metanarrative and ideological fixity and encourage an ethics that is driven by unrelenting and unending critique and a heightened awareness of the intersubjective and intertextual nature of discourse. The modernist idea of textual authority—in which an autonomous author inscribes a truth that has been revealed, intuited, or cogitated and in which that truth is imposed on the reader—is disrupted by postmodern critical ethics as it is constructed in the work of Derrida and Lyotard. Postmodern critical ethics promotes the idea that discourses are open fields of representation where meaning is worked out in the intersubjectivity and intertextuality of discursive practice.

But beyond the discursive, there is, for the postmodern perspective, no absolute system of ethics that can prescribe the appropriate and just action in every case. As Lyotard writes: "There is no knowledge in matters of ethics. And therefore there will be no knowledge in matters of politics." Instead, there is a "social web" which consists of a "multitude of encounters between interlocutors caught up in different pragmatics" (*Just Gaming* 73). No system will serve to judge each encounter before it occurs; no ultimate authoritative position exists from which to write, to value, or to judge with finality.

Foucault helped popularize the notion that the author, at least as viewed by the modernist perspective, had "disappeared." In place of the autonomous author, Foucault theorizes the position as a "certain functional principle," by which, "in our culture one limits, excludes and chooses" (352). In place of the autonomous author, Foucault

constructs the position of writer "as an ideological product . . . by
which one marks the manner in which we fear the proliferation of
meaning" (353). Thus, Foucault also sees the ethical imperative in
discourse as the one that resists authorial closure of meaning into
ideological fixity.

Lyotard reminds us that postmodern critical ethics does not promote a "rule by convention," or a reliance on the "suprasensible
nature" of humanity to arrive at common accord; nor does it argue for
the liberal rule of opinion or consensus:

> On the contrary, it rests upon something like the future of
> further inquiry: there is a free field left open to the reflective
> judgment's capability to go beyond the boundaries of sensible
> experience. (*Just Gaming* 76)

Like the best applications of critical pedagogy in composition, the
postmodern notion of critical ethics *resists* the unconscious reification
of ideological values, promotes a critical awareness of the interestedness
of discourse conventions, and emphasizes the ethical responsibilities
of situated writers and readers in their discursive encounters with the
Other.

Postmodern Ethics, Critical Pedagogy, and Resistance

Pedagogies informed by theories about how ideology is reproduced
through discursive practices are not enough in themselves to significantly alter the practices of the writing classroom. In a way, approaches based on reproductive theories merely substitute an analytic
that searches for political meaning in place of one that searches for
aesthetic meaning. Alone, the idea that discursive conventions are
political does not challenge traditional ideas of what writing can and
should accomplish; nor does it adequately address the institutions and
structures of the writing classroom. Attempts to foster critique *and*
resistance to the unconscious reification of the ideological values
promoted and reinscribed in academic, disciplinary, and cultural
discourse conventions are an improvement in that they emphasize the
value of rhetorical production and so encourage students to become
critical writers, but these pedagogies need to be further theorized by
the incorporation of postmodern critical theory and the postmodern

idea of critical ethics. Critical pedagogy informed by the postmodern idea that meaning exists only in the intertextuality and intersubjectivity of discourse allows teachers to emphasizes the openness and availability of academic, cultural, and disciplinary discourses and to address the ethical responsibility inherent in discursive activity. Once the idea is accepted that rhetoric and discourse are intimately bound up with the ethical and the political, the writing classroom becomes a place where student activity becomes an essential and meaningful part of academic, disciplinary, and cultural discourses.

The practice of critical pedagogy does not have to include the idea that students and teachers are initially naive and unaware of the interestedness of language or that unseen forces are plotting to "brainwash" naively innocent students by means of manipulative and diabolical rhetoric; nor does it promote hyper-individualism or ethics by consensus. Postmodern critical theory has much to offer composition, once it is recognized that the postmodern perspective is extremely concerned with questions of how ethics are worked out locally through intertextual, intersubjective public discourse.

The postmodern emphasis on ethics as the encounter with the Other empowers both the writer and reader and requires that those acting in both positions take renewed responsibility for their rhetorical choices and interpretations. Writing and writing instruction as viewed from the postmodern perspective are both profoundly concerned with the social, the political, and the ethical. In fact, writing pedagogy informed by postmodern critical theory should promote a heightened sense of awareness that the rhetorical conventions and genres of various discourses promote and reinscribe values and that those discourses are available to students. In addition, postmodern critical theory resists the construction of a textual authority that is attributable to an autonomous self. In its place, critical theory promotes the view that both writing and reading are political and ethical activities that require a renewed vision of how ethics operates in the scenes of writing and reading.

Postmodern critical theory supports resistance theory for the writing classroom, as both construct writing as an activity that resists ideological closure and fixity. Postmodern critical theory seeks to disrupt discursive systems and expose their openness and availability to critical writers and readers and offers an answer to the concern with whose ethical system and ideological imperative will dominate classroom practice. Under its critical eye, no ideology is allowed to attain fixity. Each interest is always questioned, always examined. From the postmodern perspective, discursive production and reception both present students and teachers with ethical responsibilities, and the classroom is revealed as a site of never-ending political and ethical contestation. Pedagogy in the politicized classroom resists the idea that writers and readers can create texts that operate free from the interestedness of the material and conceptual situations in which they are written and read.

Importantly, teachers who consider critical pedagogy from the postmodern perspective would also subject their classroom pedagogy to self-reflexive critique that would acknowledge the ethical questions raised by academic instruction in writing and reading. Writing pedagogy informed by the postmodern perspective of ethics encourages self-conscious critique of the writing class's acculturative service to academic, disciplinary, and cultural ideologies. Under the postmodern perspective, the writing classroom becomes a site where the political and ethical values represented in various discourse conventions and genres may be revealed, critiqued, accepted, and/or resisted and where the positions of author and reader come with crucial ethical responsibilities. What is most important, though, is that critical pedagogy informed by postmodern critical theory situates the student reader and writer (and the teacher) in the place where ethical responsibility and individual empowerment meet.

Chapter Four

Subjects and Power

As I outlined in Chapter Two, a primary goal of critical scholars and teachers has been to develop a writing pedagogy that contains a critique of the way discourse conventions reinforce dominant ideological values and that promotes resistance to the unconscious reification of those values. In addition, some of these same scholars have argued that, as a part of that project, the discursive and material traditions of classroom practices and the power structures that inform those traditions must also be reexamined and retheorized. To accomplish this goal, critical scholars and teachers at first proposed that classroom power structures might be realigned by a process of decentering—by shifting some of the traditional classroom authority from the teacher to the student. The goal of this type of decentering is to support the empowerment of students by encouraging them to access some of the institutional power inherent in traditional teacher functions. For example, Berlin is very specific about how these functions might be split between the teacher and students:

> While the teacher sets up the syllabus, maps out a diverse body of readings and offers methods for responding to them, students should have a choice in activities, assume leadership roles in instruction, and participate in an ongoing dialogue on the issues explored. (*Rhetorics* 135)

Beyond the empowerment of students, the aim is also to encourage compositionists to resist the reproductive nature of their own work and

of the classroom by willingly reapportioning to the students some of
the power usually associated with the teacher. The theory is, generally,
that teachers disrupt the reproductive nature of institutionalized education when they offer the students access to some of the traditional
power structures of the classroom.

Critical scholars such as Ira Shor have argued that teachers can
further decenter the power structure of the classroom by privileging
student concerns—by allowing student interests to help guide classroom content:

> Traditionally, the classroom is teacher-centered—an authori-
> tarian process for constructing authority-dependent selves.
> Critical-democratic pedagogy . . . disconfirms this dominant
> way of learning. . . . Frontloading student discourse takes the
> place of the traditional approach, which usually begins with a
> teacherly lecture about the subject matter. Instead, the students
> are asked to have an epistemic or knowledge-making relation-
> ship to the subject matter, and the teacher backloads his or her
> expertise into the way students express their understand-
> ings. . . . Thus critical pedagogy tries to position itself
> against the hegemonic culture occupying each classroom,
> school, college, and university. (Buffington and Moneyhun 3)

Shor and Berlin both advocate the idea that critical teachers should
urge students to participate in, or in some cases to perform, classroom
functions traditionally assigned to the teacher and to help set the
content of the class. Privileging students' concerns—allowing students to write about subjects that have importance in their lives or
urging them to find ways to make the content of a writing course more
relevant to their own circumstances—encourages them to resist the
"top-down" nature of traditional pedagogy. Shor describes his actions
along these lines as an attempt "to negotiate the curriculum with
students, to use my institutional authority to transform unilateral
governance into mutual authority" (Greenbaum 13). By emphasizing
critique and resistance and by encouraging students to take a more
powerful position in the classroom, critical teachers like Shor and
Berlin hope to encourage students to empower themselves within the
educational system and to resist the reproductive nature of higher
education. Shor writes that "if I pursue a critical-democratic pedagogy
that shares authority with students, I'm creating a local disruption in
the development of students into the status quo" (13).

I have chosen to highlight the role that resistance plays within these projects because resistance theories have encouraged teachers to contest both the traditional reproductive and service goals of writing and reading courses and to challenge the traditional structures of classroom power. A critique of the specifics of institutional power within the classroom is necessarily a part of critical pedagogy. If critical teachers expect to engender a critical response to the reproductive nature of higher education and to truly empower both themselves and students to resist the unconscious reification of dominant ideology, then the traditional power structures of the classroom must also become available as a topic of critique.

My contention is that resistance theories currently hold the most promise for challenging the power structure of traditional classroom activities because they suggest that there might be goals for writing instruction beyond its traditional service and acculturative roles and because resistance theories highlight the need to realign the power structures of the classroom. Still, problems reported by critical teachers suggest that critical pedagogy has not sufficiently addressed the issues of classroom authority in spite of these "decentering" activities.

In Chapters Two and Three, I argued that a discussion of values, whether addressed as issues of ideology or of ethics, is necessary and pertinent to the teaching of writing in the postmodern classroom. However, politicizing the writing classroom in this manner and making issues of value a part of the content of writing courses raises serious questions about how power is wielded in the classroom and about whose interests are best served by the projects of critical literacy—especially as regards the project to promote resistance to dominant ideology. These issues include:

1. Questions about whether classroom methods can, in fact, be consciously designed to achieve the resistance goals of critical pedagogy.

2. Questions about how those methods can serve to empower students and decenter teacher and institutional power and still work within the constraints of the contemporary academy.

3. Questions about whether some of the cultural, academic, and disciplinary interests in acculturating stu-

dents can or should be served by critical pedagogy in
the writing classroom.

4. Questions about whether the critical teacher's political
   imperatives might sometime overwhelm students' individual goals and purposes.

The major point of contention underlying each of these questions
is, as I hoped to demonstrate in Chapter One, the question of what the
content and goals of the contemporary writing course should be. Part
of my thesis in that chapter was that Romantic, Humanist, or stylistic
aesthetics are no longer adequate in and of themselves to serve as the
subject matter of composition courses; nor is the production of an
aesthetically enlightened or vocationally skilled graduate a sufficient
goal, although I believe that these traditional objectives are still useful
considerations when formulating a sound writing pedagogy. Nevertheless, in light of discussions about how discourse and language are
linked to power and cultural reproduction, it has become more apparent that compositionists can no longer simply hope that students will
learn to write and read or to become good students, professionals, and
citizens by reading canonical literature and expository essays and by
learning to write traditional student papers. Nor is it satisfactory to
adopt a skills-based approach that serves only to advance students'
careers and to ensure the business and professional sector with a
supply of workers who are adequately trained in the latest communication techniques.

My thesis is not that compositionists should abandon teaching
effective rhetoric and communication skills or neglect teaching students how to use academic and disciplinary conventions to further
their own careers as students and as professionals. However, I have
argued that writing classes should include an examination of how
discourse conventions reinscribe power structures and an analysis of
the relationship between rhetorical production and the reinscription of
or resistance to ideological values. In fact, this critical activity has
always been the underlying content of composition and writing classes,
although that activity has traditionally been used to promote a
reinscription of aesthetic, disciplinary, or professional values. The
difference now is that the idea that these values are historically and
politically interested—that they are, in fact, ideologically
overdetermined and not essential "truths"—has not been widely

considered until late. Still, teaching students that cultural, academic, and disciplinary discourses are ideologically overdetermined requires a concomitant critique of how power operates through these discourses, and that includes an examination of classroom discourses and power—what Joseph Harris calls the "micropolitics of teaching" (27).

In this chapter I will argue that the project of critical literacy has been at least partially derailed by issues of classroom power and authority, and that these issues also arise from the traditional inability to define clearly the goals of writing instruction in higher education. Then, I will examine several ways that compositionists—particularly Xin-Liu Gale and Susan Miller—have approached the need to retheorize classroom authority outside the usual projects of critical literacy.[1] Finally, I call for a discussion of classroom authority that accounts for the political nature of the relationship between the teacher, the student, and the academy and suggest that a new vocabulary may provide a way to reconsider the issue of classroom authority. This reconsideration, I will argue, could serve to revitalize the projects of critical literacy in that it would provide a way to politicize discussion of the power relationships between the student, the teacher, and the academy.

The Call to Empower Students

In each of the preceding chapters, I have concluded by advocating the empowerment of students and student writing: first, as a way to break the hold of the aesthetic and service models of composition; second, to advance the various projects of resistance suggested by critical literacy; and third, to foster a wider understanding of the link between politics, ethics, and rhetoric. The call for student empowerment is a familiar one in contemporary composition scholarship, especially among scholars of critical literacy, and not one that I would attempt to claim as original; however, critical scholars and teachers do not seem to agree on much more than the fact that the traditional classroom power structures of institutionalized education *should* be resisted. Indeed, scholars of critical literacy do not even agree on an answer to the question of whether critical literacy can finally change the power structures of the educational system in any effective way, or whether it should mainly serve as a way to subvert those structures.

Aronowitz and Giroux argue that the goal of critical pedagogy should be to foster a "language of possibility" so that schools might become places where students are taught to "exercise power over their own lives and especially over the conditions of knowledge acquisition" (*Education* xi), and yet they acknowledge that critical pedagogy has failed to provide a way to achieve this goal. Critical teachers and scholars in composition seem at times to be torn between the possibilities and successes of critical pedagogy and its limitations and failures. Knoblauch writes,

> Since teachers can only create the conditions of democratic learning, cannot compel assent to a radical agenda (except at cost to the very democracy they seek to establish), there are real boundaries to what critical teaching can accomplish. ("Critical Teaching" 19)

In addition to these problems, two features of traditional education help to make the structures of hegemonic discourse particularly impervious to resistance, and these features may serve to explain some of the problems that critical teachers face in realizing any real change through critical pedagogy. The first feature is the fact that institutions of power generally contain a prescribed space for resistance, and so they tend to incorporate and institutionalize resistant activity. In this case, real critique is contained by the fact that there is room for a great deal of dialogue in the classroom about the policies and goals of the educational system. But unless critical literacy begins to engage more openly in a discussion of the politics of the classroom in a way that moves beyond an emphasis on the dialogic, resistance could remain merely a ritualized and symbolic challenge to the hegemony of dominant ideology. The second feature that makes real change through critical pedagogy difficult to realize is the fact that there is generally an illusion of choice for those who work in culturally reproductive institutions such as the academy and for those who are subject to those institutions. Writing about the role of the radical critic, Jim Merod points out that

> radical criticism is particularly vulnerable to the superior strength of the "liberal" disciplinary state, an order that ensures its stability not by censorship or by ideological indoctrination . . . but by the structural omnipotence of relationships of force

which are masked by the appearance of the creative and freely choosing subject. (154)

In reality, critical pedagogy that both empowers students and de-centers the institutional power of the academy and the classroom has proven to be extremely elusive. The idea of a politicized, student-centered pedagogy that operates outside the aesthetic, vocational, and nationalist focuses of the nineteenth- and twentieth-century academy requires a major rethinking of the educational system and of classroom structures. Whatever course is finally chosen, it must be clear by now that if a major component of the content of composition courses is to be a study of how ideological reproduction works through rhetoric and discourse and if that study is to include an examination of how those ideologies might be reinscribed or resisted by the activity of writing, as I believe it should, then the relationship between dominant ideology and academic education in the disciplines must also become available as a topic of critique—as must a politicized discussion of the roles of both the teacher and student within this relationship. Specifically, writing instruction that employs critical pedagogy and resistance must somehow challenge the political power structures of the classroom itself. While I believe that resistance theory may finally offer such a method, more work must be done to examine how classroom power structures reinforce and can be made to resist the reproductive nature of education and about whose interests and needs are best served by pedagogical methods that teach students to resist domi-nant ideology.

Retheorizing Writing Instruction

Open admissions policies and the postmodern perspective have both been primary components in fueling the need to realign the academy within national culture—the former by forcing the academy to meet the needs of a wider diversity of students and the latter by problematizing the universalizing impulses of aestheticism and scientism as they are represented in the academic disciplines. Traditional attempts to theo-rize the role of courses in English have generally emphasized two benefits of such instruction: the first is the usefulness of these courses in training well-rounded employees who are effective communica-tors, and the second is the capacity of training in writing and reading to help unify a national culture and to support a well-informed and competent citizenry.

Attempts to emphasize the professionalizing capabilities of English instruction have generally been translated as an increased concern with teaching students to write and read within the disciplines and can be seen in classrooms that emphasize the power of writing to create and reinforce knowledge and the ability of rhetoric to perform work across the disciplines. While educators have not traditionally identified vocational training as a function of higher education, an increasingly important element in the mission of the academy has become the goal of teaching students to perform as professionals, which is in addition to an expected fluency in the content area of their studies. Elements of the various business and professional communities have been eager to suggest that writing instruction in higher education could better serve their interests by emphasizing professional training in interpersonal communication skills.

Indeed, the reaction of some English departments has been to publicly emphasize the benefits of writing classes or of the English degree for professionals who wish to highlight their communication skills. This attitude can be heard in the language of some within the English department who proudly proclaim that graduate schools and managers in professions such as law, medicine, and engineering would rather have new recruits who can communicate effectively and "write a readable memo" over those who know the content area of their discipline but who cannot communicate well. Teaching communication skills is surely an important part of the mission of the English department and of composition, and this emphasis may, in fact, be the best way to assure the survival of the English department. Nevertheless, the return to an emphasis on writing and reading as vocational tools would only signal a retrogression to service models of composition and could make critical pedagogy, with its postmodern emphasis on the political nature and critical uses of writing, irrelevant. Additionally, business and professional communication has generally evolved outside the influence of the academy, and so English departments are already years behind in the development and understanding of business and professional communication (Russell 105).

Attempts to emphasize culturally unifying benefits of education in reading and writing can be seen in the recent calls for a return to the traditions of style and canon as a way to stress the normalizing power of a "national discourse." These attempts to readdress the acculturative nature of higher education by emphasizing the unifying effect of a standard body of cultural and aesthetic knowledge have produced very narrow and prescriptive views of how the academy might promote national unity. The most notorious of these attempts, such as that promoted by E.D. Hirsch, have been roundly criticized for their foundationalism and for their prescriptive nature.[2]

This emphasis is also apparent in the recent turn toward cultural studies as a way to make the department more relevant to mainstream culture and to make the content of English courses more accurately reflect students' lives outside the academy. The acceptance of cultural studies is, I believe, part of the project to assure the survival of the English department in the postmodern, multi-cultural academy in that it is an attempt to make the academy more relevant to popular and diverse cultures and to make those cultures a part of academic study. While cultural studies certainly does help to make the content of English courses more relevant, it does not represent an adequate realignment of educational goals for the writing and reading classroom, as I hoped to show in Chapter One. The use of texts other than those of the traditional canon does, in fact, broaden the scope of the English class; however, by itself cultural studies does not break the hold of academic aestheticism and its universalizing impulses; nor does it fully address the need to restructure the hierarchies of academic and classroom power.[3]

These attempts to retheorize the place of the English department— as a place to teach professional communication skills or as a place to teach a unifying or more relevant aesthetic—fall well short of the need to realign the academy in a way that will support training in composition into the next century, at least without turning the writing class into a skills workshop or into a tool of nationalist, vocational, or radical acculturation. Additionally, I believe that few administrators and fewer scholars and teachers want to abandon completely the traditions of English disciplinarity for the study of mainstream culture or to turn the academy over to the direction of corporate interests; nevertheless, the academy can no longer stand apart from mainstream culture and will, I think, be forced increasingly to justify its activities to the interests of corporate, government, and mainstream culture, even as it is pressured to make its content more relevant to a wider variety of students. These pressures present the academy and the English department with serious problems; however, they also present great potential for the study of writing and reading to include a discussion of how cultural and academic discourses reinscribe power relationships.

Before open admissions, the English department perhaps had the luxury of focusing on strictly aesthetic concerns, but as higher education has become more prevalent, and therefore more relevant, the business and professional sectors have rightly advocated an increased role for higher education in training workers to perform specific job skills. Additionally, students and teachers have appropriately called for the content and methods of academic courses to address students' material and cultural needs more directly—the needs of an increasingly diverse student body. These are also new issues for higher education, and they have come to be issues because of the realization that higher education plays a key role in the reproduction of national, social, disciplinary, and cultural ideologies.

Critical Pedagogy and the Role of the Teacher

Responding to the need to retheorize and realign classroom power structures, scholars and teachers of critical literacy have endeavored to rethink the specific role that the writing teacher plays in the reproduction of dominant ideology. Revelations about the political nature of classroom activity and calls for student empowerment have necessitated a reconsideration of the roles of both the writing student and the writing teacher, but questions remain about whether critical pedagogy can actually challenge or change the traditions of teacher authority in any significant way. Scholars of critical pedagogy such as Shor and Berlin have called for teachers to decentralize classroom power, but the entrenched traditions of the classroom have made any reapportionment of classroom authority extremely problematic. Lad Tobin has pointed out that too often these initial attempts to decenter classroom power ignore or fail to consider adequately how deeply traditional power structures are embedded within the traditions of the classroom and underestimate the ability of these traditions to absorb and institutionalize resistance. Resisting the traditional power structures of the classroom is not as simple as refusing to take on an authoritative role. Tobin believes that too many critical compositionists simply deny their classroom authority because it does not fit with the image they would like to project. Most of us are uncomfortable admitting that we are the center of a "de-centered" classroom, that we hold so much power, that we are largely responsible for success and, even worse, failure. But while there are good reasons for our discomfort—many of us would like for political reasons to think of our classroom as democratic, supportive, and non-hierarchical—there are even better reasons to face the truth: from a student's perspective a writing teacher *is* an authority figure. (338)

While the critical teacher may release authority in such areas as leading discussion and setting course goals and content, he or she will often find that students' and the academy's expectations continue to reinforce traditional power structures in spite of these tactics. As a result of these expectations, critical teachers have reported various difficulties in their attempts to re-align the power structures of their own classes.

Scholars of critical literacy such as Knoblauch have posited that one of the reasons for this difficulty may be that much of the theory behind critical pedagogy in America has emerged primarily from the work of Paulo Freire, whose work is connected with literacy programs in South America. Knoblauch and others have pointed out that the literacy problems in these situations are very different from those encountered by critical teachers in America. For example, the conditions of profound illiteracy that fueled Freire's work in Brazil were the result of a massive institutional oppression by a cruel and indifferent ruling elite. Since conditions of literacy in the US do not easily resolve into such a stark contrast, it is reasoned that the application of critical literacy must also be more subtle here.

In working out these problems, critical scholars such as Shor, Giroux, Berlin, and Knoblauch have argued that the project of critical literacy in America is primarily intended to support the educational efforts of marginalized students: students who lack "basic" literacy skills, women, those from ethnic minorities traditionally excluded from higher education, and those from socio-economic classes not traditionally served by post-secondary schools. Knoblauch writes,

The goal has been to find ways to enfranchise "outsiders," typically by making them more aware of the means by which power is gained, used, and distributed in the professional and other communities they may wish to enter; more aware of the

ways simultaneously to acquire that power and also subvert the
structures that objectify prevailing, and debilitating, power
arrangements. (15)

Still, critical teachers often complain that these liberatory goals are
derailed by the students themselves. In one such instance, Shor
describes how his own classes reacted to his empowering techniques
by ignoring his attempts to "frontload" student concerns into the
content of his class and instead moving to subvert the most elemental
and fundamental of classroom power structures: grades and tests
(*When Students* 82). While Shor is initially taken aback by his
students' interest in what he considers the more mundane issues of
evaluation and grading, this action, in fact, shows that his students are
all-too-keenly aware of the authoritarian nature of classroom politics.
The problem is that Shor finds himself in a situation that is very much
like the one in which his students find themselves: "Shor, like the
students, is held under the rule of an authoritarian system that under-
mines his best attempts to empower the students and decenter the
teacher"; at times it seems that the students intuitively understand this
better than does the critical teacher (Hardin 528).

Critical pedagogy has yet to adequately address the fact that
student desires and needs often are very much at odds with the aims
and methods of the critical teacher. Additionally, if critical pedagogy
is to survive in the American classroom, it must more adequately
address the way classroom authority is constructed, and it must do so
in a way that resists becoming "institutionalized" resistance. Jim
Merod writes,

> Critical work cannot be thought of as distant from the central
> assumptions that orient all other institutions. Everything in the
> social field is permeated by power's strategies. The irony here
> for "normal" freely creative critics who mean to exercise
> interpretive skill, as for "radical" critics who intend to influ-
> ence the institutional force of the schools or fields in which they
> work, is the unconscious cooperation everyone lends to the
> stability of the reigning order. (155)

While Merod's comments are directed primarily toward literary critics, the same caution holds true for those of us who work in composition. Subverting the power structures that have been built into the
Western classroom since its beginnings will not be easy.

Challenging the Traditions of Authority

If the postmodern perspective directs scholars away from the search for truths that might be universal and unassailable, then that turn also has dire consequences for teachers, whose authority traditionally has been based on the possession and control of intellectual power. However, the figure of the intellectual, like the site of writing instruction, has now been politicized and must be radically reconstructed in ways that will have great consequences for the position of the teacher. First, those who work within the academy can no longer claim to be in possession of knowledge and truths that are absolute and unassailable; however, neither must they be bound any longer within elite disciplinary and class structures. The academy and its disciplines are no longer isolated and insulated worlds, and this is especially true of composition, which has the potential to influence knowledge-making outside the academy and across the disciplines. Increasingly, scholars and teachers of composition have been asked to engage writing pedagogy in a way that serves students from widely diverse class and ethnic origins and to teach those students to make rhetoric work across a wider variety of situations and disciplines.

As Foucault writes, the idea of the "universal" intellectual, who works in the arena of ecumenical truth, has given way to the idea of the "specific" intellectual, whose work is more locally specific and "whose specificity is linked, in a society like ours, to the general functioning of an apparatus of truth" ("Truth" 73). The idea of the intellectual "who spoke and was acknowledged the right of speaking in the capacity of master of truth and justice" is no longer useful, at least from the postmodern perspective (67). Instead,

> a new mode of the "connection between theory and practice" has been established. Intellectuals have become used to working, not in the modality of the "universal," the "exemplary," and the "just-and-true-for all," but within specific sectors, at the precise points where their own conditions of life or work situate them. (67-68)

However, these same conditions have made it possible for those who teach rhetoric and discourse production to move laterally across disciplines, and this also serves to politicize the position of the writing teacher. Working from Foucault's idea of the "specific" intellectual,

Goleman writes that by

> reconnecting the traditionally transcendent values of knowl-
> edge and truth to worldly networks of power relations that are
> materialized in discourse, Foucault, by implication, puts tradi-
> tional approaches to composition (and its assumptions about
> knowledge) under radical review. (2)

Indeed, the traditional authority of the teacher, which was based on the
institutional certification that he or she was master of the discipline,
has been critically challenged by the postmodern perspective.

Xin Liu Gale points out in *Teachers, Discourses and Authority in
the Postmodern Composition Classroom* that critical scholars' "in-
quiry into the politics of the dominant discourse has truly touched
upon the foundation of the traditional authority of the teacher" (3). For
Gale, critical literacy has, in fact, broken new and useful ground in the
project to retheorize teacher authority in that it has revealed how "the
teacher's discourse embodies the ideology of the dominant culture and
reflects all the privileges the dominant class enjoys and all the
disadvantages the underclasses suffer" (3). Nevertheless, Gale points
out that privileging the discourses of students over the discourse of the
academy, as critical pedagogy has attempted to do, does little to
change the traditions of teacher authority. Instead, Gale seems to
accept the inevitability of teacher authority and, instead, proposes a
new use for that authority. Gale argues,

> alone, critical teachers' attempts to substitute for the canon a
> new canon or to replace the teaching of the dominant discourse
> with the teaching of radical discourses do not prevent the
> teacher's authority from being oppressive and exclusive. (4)

Gale is adamant that teachers cannot simply "choose to abandon
the institutional authority that oppresses students and reproduces
inequality"; nor can they subvert the power of institutional authority
simply by exercising liberatory and democratic pedagogy in their own
personal classrooms (34). The problem, as Gale seems to see it, is that
the institutionalized authority of the academy as it is enacted upon the
students cannot be subverted by the simple interposition of a critical
teacher between the student and the institution. Instead, Gale employs
Richard Rorty's notion of normal and abnormal discourse to propose

that teachers use their authority in the classroom to act as "edifying agents."

Rorty has proposed that normal discourse can be disrupted by the interposition of abnormal discourse. Normal discourse, as defined by Rorty, is "that which is conducted within an agreed-upon set of conventions about what counts as a relevant contribution" (320). Abnormal discourse is more difficult to define. Abnormal discourse is not merely an alternative to normal discourse and does not seek to replace normal discourse. Instead, abnormal discourse

> exists for the purpose of keeping the conversation from closing down and keeping discourses from perpetuating themselves as normal discourse. Abnormal discourse does not seek knowledge or truth but renders new descriptions through wisdom; it does not intend to engender new normal discourse or competing paradigms. (Gale 69)

Gale argues that there are actually three discourses active in the classroom: "the students's discourse(s), the teacher's discourse, and the dominant discourse" (5). Adapting and expanding Rorty's language, Gale defines these discourses: student's discourse is generally defined as non-responsive abnormal discourse; the teacher's discourse is defined as responsive abnormal discourse; and the discourse of the academy (or of the discipline, or of the nation) is defined as normal discourse. In her scheme, teachers participate in two levels of interaction: between non-responsive abnormal discourse (student discourse) and normal discourse, and between non-responsive abnormal discourse and responsive abnormal discourse.

Initially, the teacher encourages students to interact with normal discourse. Gale argues that it is important for students, who are "outsiders speaking non-responsive abnormal discourse," to encounter normal discourse as it is embodied in the disciplinary texts and language of the academy (107). This encounter serves as

> a means and a force to help students break away from the restrictions of their home discourse and the existing stabilized social audience, as they become acquainted with the new discourse and the new social audience it addresses. (107)

Normal discourse emphasizes knowledge and how meaning is made and represented. It also demonstrates how meaning and knowledge is circulated, perceived, and employed. The dissonances produced by the interaction between the student's own discourse and the discourse of the culture, the academy, or the disciplines can be employed to develop an understanding of the interested and social nature of discourse in general and of the acculturative and constructed character of these discourses specifically. Gale writes that "to interact with normal discourse means to interact with the dominant ideology" (115).

Gale theorizes another interaction between students' non-responsive abnormal discourse and the responsive abnormal discourse of the teacher, which functions to resist the oppressive and exclusive nature of normal discourse and which "functions as a critical and empowering force in the classroom" (116). The secondary interaction

> keeps a watchful eye of normal discourse's authority lest it becomes silencing, for responsive abnormal discourse knows well how the institutional constraints can intimidate and oppress those from the underprivileged communities. Because responsive abnormal discourse is capable of seeing through the hidden ideologies of normal discourse as well as its biases and interests, it interacts with non-responsive abnormal discourse to resist the normal discourse's claim of neutrality, scientificity, and disinterestedness. (118).

Working still from Rorty, and specifically from his idea of the "edifying philosopher," Gale proposes the concept of the "edifying teacher." This position, like the position of the edifying philosopher, resists metanarratives and discourses of truth and rationality, and supports a dialogic, hermeneutic relationship with students. The edifying teacher, like the critical teacher, is willing to reexamine how cultural, academic, and disciplinary ideologies are reproduced through normal discourse and rejects the claim that the values promoted by these discourses are foundationally and universally true. Importantly, Gale's construction of the edifying teacher also explores the obligations to institution and culture inherent in the role of teacher, which is an analysis that much critical pedagogy does not address in a significant way. While the edifying teacher employs normal discourse to teach the power of knowledge and rhetoric and to disrupt the non-responsive abnormal discourse of the student, edifying pedagogy does not "consider acculturation and accommodation or the mastery of normal discourse the ultimate goal of teaching writing" (129). While the goal of critical teachers has often been to emancipate, liberate, or transform students, the edifying teacher is hyper-sensitive to the effect that the teacher's political agenda might have on the students and works to make the rhetoric and conventions of cultural, academic, and disciplinary discourse available sites for student articulation.

As Susan Miller knowingly points out in *Rescuing the Subject*, students' first attempts at writing and reading academic texts often reveal just how arbitrary discourse conventions actually are. In their attempts to get the text to "sound right," writing students offer compositionists a glimpse of our own assumptions about what makes good text:

> Their writing leaves us unable to ignore the discourse-as-discourse quality of our own writing and equally unable to reject a theory that tries to acknowledge its multiply voiced and distinct communities. Language speaks through them. They are without our defenses, filters, and conscious processes of selection, or, better, of metaselection. . . . This writing shows how two-edged "convention" is, how it inevitably contains us before we become free, only provisionally, to use it within a well-marked field of play. Basic writers also, therefore, know conventions better than we do. By virtue of their innocent certainty about being able to learn to write—to directly originate and further to "communicate" in writing—basic writers call into question what we have meant and may mean by authorship. (169)

The space of writing, as it is occupied by the student making his or her first attempts at academic discourse, reminds us that discourse conventions are, at best, unstable and arbitrary and, at worst, oppressive and dominating: "They write as if—despite, and in the face of writing itself" (170).

In *Textual Carnivals*, Miller argues that the project to empower students within the writing classroom is hopeless without a "redefinition of student writing and of the subjectivity of the student writer" that challenges the traditions of writing instruction (191). These traditions, as they have been discussed elsewhere in these pages and by so many other compositionists, have constructed the entire project of composition—its teachers, its students, and the texts produced by *both*—as somehow inferior. In spite of the gains made in legitimizing the study and teaching of writing, a great deal of academic and mainstream cultural thought still considers composition primarily in its vocational or acculturative roles. Composition research is not "real" research; composition teachers are not "real" teachers; composition students do not write "real" texts. In addition to the legitimizing of composition teachers and research, Miller writes that "the identity of the student in teaching, research, and administrative practices offers a key to the politics of composition" (*Rescuing* 196).

Too often, the academy and compositionists have cast writing students variously as discursive naives who need to be acculturated into the discourse conventions of the academy or of national culture, as individuals stuck somewhere within their own cognitive processes, or as those who need to learn the skills necessary only to write well enough to succeed within a discipline or a profession. Compositionists have arrived at the point where further advancement requires that student writers and writing teachers be retheorized within the vital political positions they occupy. Writing, as I have tried to demonstrate, is the emblematic site of postmodern politics and ethics, and there is the sense that composition sits at the intersection of a multiplicity of interests—individual, communal, institutional, cultural, national, and global. Student writers and writing classes offer a rare opportunity to examine the nature of discursive fields as they come into conflict with each other and to examine how these fields are constructed. Additionally, if student writing could be considered seriously for what it reveals about academic, disciplinary, and cultural discourses, then it could hold the promise of generating new knowledge within those fields. Unfortunately, the examination of student texts is still largely done only to sort and evaluate students:

> What is needed additionally is the articulation and critique . . .
> disclosing connections between specific social and textual
> superstructures and highlighting how writing situations construct their participant writers before, during, and after they
> undertake any piece of writing. Without this additional reflexivity in pedagogical and theoretical accounts, the student's
> writing is left in its self-contained world of textual features,
> where its consequences are already limited to intransitive
> matters of "quality." (Miller, *Textual* 198)

Toward a Political Theory of Classroom Authority

Theorists such as Gale and Miller seem to recognize that it is not enough to reduce the power relationship between student and teacher to a communicative one. As Bourdieu has pointed out, to do so "would make it impossible to account for the specific characteristics it owes to the authority of the pedagogic institution" (108-09). Still, there must be some way out of the notion that the authority of the institution will always expand to encompass whatever disruption the critical teacher can engender. I contend that that way lies with yet an increased sense of the political in composition pedagogy—with a view toward writing instruction that places the writer and instruction in discourse at the center of postmodern politics. The positions of student writer and of writing teacher are emblematic constructions of the political, institutional machinery that has served to reinscribe the dominant ideology of national culture (at least in the U.S.) for the last 250 years. As such, the power structures of the writing classroom should not be reduced to personality or individual politics but should be expanded to include the basic issues of discursive power.

Plainly, resistance theory has opened up the subject of classroom authority and has identified the writing classroom as emblematic of the way cultural and academic power is reinscribed through discourse and language. Nevertheless, critical pedagogy has seemingly reached somewhat of a standstill in its project to "liberate" and "emancipate" students. Compositionists such as Gale and Miller have moved discussion about the nature of classroom authority beyond the purely dialogic and personal levels, and their work is valuable in that it further reveals the importance of the student-teacher relationship in the writing classroom to an understanding of educational politics.

Still, the methods of critical pedagogy can do much to disrupt the specific power configurations of the academy and of culture, at least as they are localized within the classroom. Such strategies as refraining from lecturing, refusing to adopt the magisterial air of the traditional teacher, putting the chairs in a circle, coming out from behind the desk, and allowing familiarity *do* decenter classroom power and begin a movement toward student empowerment. Encouraging students to set the content of the class and to control how evaluation is accomplished can do more. Still, unless student activities can be seen to have some relevance beyond the classroom, then they remain "merely" rhetorical.

Gale's idea of the "edifying" teacher does present a way for critical teachers to work within the traditional acculturative role of the academy and to encourage critique and resistance to the normalization of cultural and academic values at the same time. Teachers, even critical teachers, must still perform a gatekeeper role, and abdicating that role is not likely to change much about the way cultural values are reproduced through educational conventions. Abdicating the gatekeeper role is also likely to seem artificial to students. Nevertheless, as critical teachers disclose their own work as gatekeepers in the classroom, they do call that role into question and so can encourage students to examine the acculturative role of education for themselves. Gale's construction of the "edifying" teacher suggests that the teacher can work both to give students a hand at joining in the conversations of culture and the academy and at the same time work to disrupt that reproduction. Miller's insistence that student texts be seen as more than a way to evaluate their readiness does even more. Students must be encouraged to see their texts as viable intercessions into academic and cultural discourse. Further moves to make student texts more obviously useful may include service learning and more publication outlets for these texts. At the very least, assignments must give students a sense of actual authorship.

Composition is precisely situated at a significant point of contestation within the changes that now confront the academy. Issues of content, purpose, value, and authority confront the department with new and imposing challenges, but they also present the department with a way to make the academy, and especially the study of rhetorical production and reception, more relevant and more likely to have an impact on mainstream culture.

Chapter Five

Resistance, Emancipation, and Hybridity

While this text has dealt variously with issues of aestheticism and culture, resistance and reproduction, poststructuralist ethics and classroom power structures, my focus throughout has been generally on resistance theory and the projects of critical pedagogy. I have been interested most specifically in how resistance theory has been employed by critical teachers in the attempt to empower students by teaching them to resist the unthinking acceptance of ideological values as they are presented in the various discourses of the academy and of culture.

As I have suggested in several places throughout this text, the tensions that surface whenever questions arise about whether teaching resistance can and should be a goal of writing instruction indicate that resistance theory has a key role to play in the project to realign composition studies so that it serves more than just an acculturative role in society and more than just a service role in the academy. Equally important to the future of composition studies, and even less easily answered, are specific questions about how resistance can be employed most successfully to promote critical writing in the classroom in a way that challenges the acculturative and vocational aims of education without negating the legitimate need to teach students conventional language skills.

My own review of pertinent literature on the subjects of critical literacy, critical pedagogy, and resistance theory leads me to think that scholars and teachers of critical pedagogy have had some significant success in drawing attention to the way the discourses of culture and of the academy serve to reinforce the hegemony of dominant cultural and academic ideologies; however, more needs to be done to establish just how that knowledge can be translated into effective writing pedagogy. In my estimation, research in critical literacy and critical pedagogy has at least contributed to the growing awareness among students, teachers, and scholars that textual representations and rhetorical choices always serve some ideological agenda. Still, critical teachers who have attempted to formulate classroom practices that promote resistance have not yet fully reconciled the role of resistance theory and critical pedagogy in the academy. In fact, those who are committed to the projects of critical literacy often report as many failures as successes in their attempts to adapt resistance theory and critical pedagogy to their classroom practices, and much recent criticism has been aimed at those failures by those who are unsure about the efficacy of critical pedagogy and by those who are more or less opposed to the projects of critical pedagogy in the first place.[1]

Scholars of critical literacy have come a long way in helping to promote the idea that the national project of higher education is unquestionably political, and that composition, because it is concerned with how ideological values are articulated through rhetoric, is ideally situated to lead a discussion of the ways in which language and power intersect in the discourses of both the academy and of culture. Indeed, scholars working within the general area of critical literacy have done much to advance the argument that there are unmistakable links between rhetoric and politics, between rhetoric and hegemony, and between rhetoric and the construction of individual and group ethics and identity. Further, researchers in critical literacy and pedagogy have helped foreground the normative function of disciplinary, academic, and cultural discourse conventions and have promoted the possibility that schools and teachers might do more than simply serve to acculturate and normalize students into dominant cultural or disciplinary ideologies.

I must admit that these successes may, at times, seem like painfully small steps in a very slow process, but I think that the implications are large for those of us who work in English studies. After all, an acceptance of the link between discourse and power seems to demand at least some rethinking of pedagogy in the English department, and this reconsideration would seem to require that writing and reading pedagogy now include a consideration of the political effects of teaching students to critique and resist or to accept and naturalize various cultural and disciplinary ideologies. At the very least, many scholars and teachers who have engaged the projects of critical literacy have attempted to meet these challenges. Still, critical teachers have reported significant difficulty in translating an awareness of the ideologically reproductive nature of education into classroom practices that can empower students within academic and cultural discourses, that can liberate them from uncritical consumerism and conformity, and that can teach them to resist the unthinking acceptance of hegemonic values. While it might be easy to diminish the successes of critical teachers in "liberating" large numbers of individuals, scholars and teachers of critical pedagogy have unquestionably succeeded on at least two fronts: they have promoted productive dialogue about how the normative functions of academic and cultural discourses operate, and they have promoted active discussion about the possibility that students and teachers might be taught to critique and resist the unconscious reification of cultural and disciplinary values.

I think that these successes indicate that the basic impulses that drive critical literacy and pedagogy are sound; however, I also think that there is a great deal of theoretical work to do if scholars and teachers of critical pedagogy are to develop instructional practices that make full use of the knowledge that the control of language and representation are key to ideological hegemony and personal and group identity. I also am concerned that recent criticisms of critical pedagogy and resistance theory have tempted some teachers and scholars to turn away from these projects and have created some ambivalence about their usefulness. At the very least, some of these criticisms do seem to be cause for another look at the formulations of critical literacy and pedagogy.

In this last chapter, I hope to address a few of these particular lines of critique. My hope is that by examining these criticisms, I might help point the way to a rethinking of what it means to teach resistance. Specifically, I want to examine how we might rethink our goals of "liberating" and "empowering" students. Additionally, I will argue that scholars of critical literacy and critical teachers might help the cause of critical pedagogy by engaging a more fully theorized understanding of how the act of writing serves to construct the very ground of political and cultural resistance and by examining how writing instruction in the academy can help to promote the idea that cultural, academic, and disciplinary discourses are open, available, and useful sites where critical students and teachers can engage the values and ideas of the academy and of culture. First, I want to examine a few of the recent criticisms that have been aimed at the projects of critical literacy and critical pedagogy and look at how they might suggest more complex and useful critique.

The Critique of Freire

In a recent article in *College English* based on his analysis of why critical teachers have been less than completely successful in developing their pedagogy, Richard E. Miller poses what appears to be a "rhetorical" question. He asks, "When you teach composition, are you working for the system or against it?" (25). Miller uses the question as a springboard for his argument, which is, finally, that compositionists can and must work both inside and outside of the system. However, Miller's article is most useful, I think, not for what it says about the future of critical pedagogy but for the clear and coherent way it outlines the popular criticisms of resistance theory and critical pedagogy.

The first of these criticisms focuses on the fact that compositionists are faced with subjects who have different needs, desires, and goals than did the original subjects of Freirean pedagogy. In one version of this criticism, it is reasoned that composition teachers' subjects, unlike Freire's, do not need to be liberated because they are not oppressed, at least not in the ways that Freire's subjects were oppressed. Another version of this same criticism argues that the majority of writing students in America generally *want* to be acculturated into cultural and disciplinary ideologies and that critical teachers do a disservice to these students by undermining their legitimate goals.

Along the same line, more cynical writers (and some frustrated critical teachers) have reasoned that American students may already be so acculturated by the time they reach post-secondary composition classes that what they actually resist most is the idea that they should devote any of their valuable time in the academy to questioning and resisting the values of a mainstream culture whose major ideologies they largely embrace and support. Miller articulates a version of this criticism in his article:

Freire, as previously noted, wasn't concerned with teaching first-year college students the nuances of academic prose or the virtues of the expository essay. His work was with illiterate peasants who were struggling to combat their government's oppressive policies. . . . It would be foolish to equate the challenges Freire has confronted in the field . . . with the challenges we face teaching composition in the academy: we teach those who have already found their way into the system, those who wish, at some level, to gain access to the material benefits that higher education is said to promise. (18)

Scholars who employ this line of criticism often suggest that most composition students, at least those who are not members of a group that has been specifically marginalized by the academy or by mainstream culture, are actually already "junior members" of the managerial class. As I have noted in previous chapters, some critics have reasoned that the educational needs of these students are, then, diametrically opposed to the goals of critical literacy and pedagogy. Unless the composition teacher is faced with a classroom that contains only students from marginalized groups, it *is* hard for many critics to imagine how the methods of critical pedagogy could serve all the students' needs. Even then, it is sometimes reasoned that the best way to empower marginalized students is to give them the language tools they will need in order to succeed within the managerial class.

A second area of criticism focuses on the notion that critical pedagogy operates on a system that constructs a binary of "false" and "authentic" consciousness. This criticism argues that critical teachers believe that their students, like Freire's peasants, labor under a veil of ideology that can only be lifted by the interposition of a "liberatory" pedagogy. Critics have charged that this is an elitist attitude that privileges the world view of the teacher while masking his or her actual power within the classroom. Critics like Miller charge that this formulation constructs the student as a naive or misled innocent:

Indeed, I would argue that the prevailing desire to re-construct the scene of instruction as a site where authenticity is forged and layers of false consciousness are peeled away indicates a general commitment in our profession to imagining that the power dynamic in the teacher-student relationship can, under ideal conditions, be erased. (19)

This critique suggests that critical teachers labor under a snobbish assumption that students' values and ideas are primarily the result of their unthinking acceptance of cultural representations constructed and reinforced by mass media or learned at home. It also suggests that critical teachers, in their attempts to let student concerns control classroom content, wrongfully abandon, neglect, mis-recognize, or conceal their authoritative roles as teachers. Critics have charged, and perhaps rightly so in some cases, that critical teachers are guided by a inherent elitism, which supposes that until a student has been taught to critically examine the ideological values embedded in cultural and academic discourses he or she cannot be liberated from the "incorrect" ideas supported by his or her own false consciousness.

Miller's critique in this case also indicates the way to the third major criticism: that the imposition of critical pedagogy is but another oppression of students—this time by the radical project of the critical teacher. In this line of critique, practitioners of critical pedagogy are chastised for deploying their own leftist world view in a way that oppresses students or silences those voices that might dissent from the teacher's liberatory project. While this failing is not traced exclusively to Freire, Miller again uses Freire as his example of how critical pedagogy often puts the goals of the teacher ahead of those of the students:

> Freire presents the recipients of his pedagogy as coming to their own conclusions, as learning to think for themselves. He doesn't linger over the fact that all this self-motivated thinking leads his students to think exactly what he would like them to think; he doesn't imagine that, possibly, his students are mouthing his pieties, silently collaborating in the production of the desired public transcript and then sneaking back home where they are free to question his lessons or force others to accept them or forget them altogether. (19)

This criticism suggests that critical pedagogy either forces students to accept the critical world view of the teacher as the correct world view, or that critical teachers merely reinforce students' suspicions that the way to achieve high marks and success in the academy is to mimic the views of the teacher.

Again, my purpose here is not specifically to defend Freire, critical literacy, or liberatory and resistance pedagogy from these distinct criticisms. Freire has already answered in print that most of these criticisms are the result of a naive reading of his work, and that is a reply that I would humbly support.[2] In the first case, the argument that our composition students are not oppressed in the same ways or to the same degree that Freire's subjects were seems to miss the point. Undoubtedly, the specifics of critical pedagogy as it was practiced by Freire are most usefully contextualized within the conditions of Brazil during the economic crisis that plagued that country in the 1970s, as any specific pedagogy might be best understood if localized within the specifics of its original formulation. However, the argument that critical literacy programs and critical pedagogy based on a Freirean model have generally failed in America because they are out of context is too glibly made. It is true that the gap between rich and poor in America is not yet as vast as the one that Freire saw in Brazil during the 1970s. Likewise, American democracy has not yet given way completely to a corporatized oligarchy that could rival the political situation that has ravaged Brazil and much of South America for the last hundred years. Still, in many vital ways, I would argue that our students, should they not be encouraged to question and resist the ideological formulations of the academy and of culture, are subject to just the same sort of state and cultural domination that made economic slaves or outcasts out of significant populations of Brazilian peasants during Freire's time. Before we begin to quibble about degrees of oppression or to reassure ourselves that the social, cultural, and economic struggles in America and on its campuses will forever be expressed only as *pedagogic* violence, or to imagine that only a certain portion of our students—ethnic and religious minorities, working class students, and women, specifically—are *marginalized* (a much nicer word than *oppressed*), we would do well to remember just how fast the distance between America's richest and poorest citizens is growing and just how quickly some elements of our own government were willing to turn the force of the police and the national guard on the campus protesters of the 1960s and 1970s and the civil rights protesters of the 1950s and 1960s. Indeed, the struggles for racial, gender, and economic equality in this country have each arisen from circumstances that can only be called oppressive. Only recently have the institutions of American culture acknowledged the right of women, minorities, and the working class to have access to the economic choices and potentials offered by higher education. In fact, current moves to dismantle affirmative action policies indicate that these groups may be losing ground in their struggle for mainstream cultural and academic representation and for the economic opportunities offered by the institutions of higher education.

I am just as certain, however, that many of our students enter the academy already prepared to assume their places among the managerial class, and that *these* students may not wish to be liberated from anything. In fact, these students often react to critical pedagogy by adopting a resistant posture against the entire liberatory project of the critical teacher. As much as we may want to help these students achieve their vocational goals, I think that once we have acknowledged the political nature of our own work we can never return to the innocent and supposedly apolitical neutrality of service and vocational models of writing instruction. If we believe that we can ever teach without working some kind of pedagogical violence on our charges and without supporting some kind of political agenda, then we have learned nothing about the way power operates through discourse, especially through the powerful acculturative forces of the academy. This is where teachers must choose their *own* points of resistance.

At the very least, critical and liberatory pedagogies have promoted the idea that teachers should recognize and disclose the nature of their own political agendas. As I have pointed out in other chapters, critical pedagogy, if it is practiced with care and respect, does not have to require students to accept that the teacher's world view, whatever that may be, is the only correct one. While critical teachers can promote the idea that students should resist the unthinking acceptance of ideological values, they can also point out that students have the choice to accept or resist those values according to their own sense of what is right and what is wrong.

Still, the projects of critical literacy and critical pedagogy do need further critique. However, the failures of critical pedagogy are not, I think, because its goals and methods cannot be successfully contextualized within the American educational landscape. Instead, these disappointments might be traced to the fact that critical scholars and teachers have often failed to fully embrace poststructuralist thought and the postmodern turn and are still laboring under ideas of liberation and emancipation that issue directly from the master narratives of modernity.

Part of what has made critical pedagogy particularly vulnerable to critique is the failure of critical teachers and scholars to historicize adequately their own emancipatory projects and to shift the ground of their arguments away from the old disagreements between which ideology—that of the political left or that of the political right—points the way to social and individual emancipation. Instead of launching another self-reflexive critique of critical literacy and critical pedagogy based on the specific charges delineated so well in Miller's article, which all center on how critical pedagogy has failed in the classroom, I would like to see a radical revisioning and historicizing of the emancipatory project of critical literacy and a more thorough theorization of how the act of writing enacts political and cultural resistance and constructs individual and group identities. The first move might include a thorough examination of critical literacy's roots in the desire to see education as the emancipator of its subject. The second might focus on how the act of writing serves to hybridize and rearticulate discursive conventions and the ideological values they support. To this end, I want to begin, here at the end of my project, to suggest how these two lines of thinking might help push critical scholars and teachers beyond their reliance on Freirean and neo-Marxist theories of reproduction and resistance and toward a more active engagement with theories of hegemony and social democracy drawn from postmodern, poststructuralist, and postcolonial thought.

The Politics of Liberation

I would agree with Freire that criticisms such as those made by Miller are based largely on reductive readings of the goals and methods of critical pedagogy. Nevertheless, these criticisms do point the way, I think, to more complex critiques of the projects of critical literacy and critical pedagogy—critiques that emphasize how critical theories and practices have not been able to escape modernist notions of emancipation. In view of this concern, those who wish to make more complex critiques might first concern themselves with how scholars and teachers of critical literacy and critical pedagogy too often partake of Enlightenment arguments about which set of universals offers humanity (or in this case, students) the best chance for achieving a utopic and unified social structure or a "liberated" and "empowered" self.

Critical teachers are often cited, as in Miller's article, for their expressed goal of "liberating" students from the structures of traditional schooling. Here, critical teachers might be legitimately criticized for substituting merely another moral sense of what the goals of education ought to be. As I have noted, in this critique the critical teacher is usually accused of promoting his or her own goals for education in place of traditional goals or for substituting some other world view (usually Marxist or feminist) in place of traditional (usually vocational or acculturative) world views. Formulated in this way, critical literacy *would* simply seem to be an oppositional discourse—merely one of two competing views of what the goals of education should be, each arguing that its application points the way to the proper education of students, and, in some cases, to the salvation of the democratic social order. Although critical teachers and scholars in America have tended to accentuate the critical aspects of Freirean liberatory pedagogy, there is little question that the projects of critical literacy and critical pedagogy often have been constructed in direct opposition to the goals of reproductive or service models of education. In this case, it is easy to see how some could criticize these projects as merely substituting one world view for another. Indeed, critical literacy is constructed by many of its most visible proponents as an oppositional discourse to an "other" discourse about the goals of education. This formulation is often evident, for example, in the writings of Giroux:

> Academics and cultural workers must redefine the purpose of higher education not as a servant of the state nor to meet the demands of commerce and the marketplace but as a repository for educating students and others in the democratic discourse of freedom, social responsibility, and public leadership. ("Racial" 195)

In Giroux's construction, there are two possible goals for education: to acculturate and normalize students or to liberate them from the oppression of the state and the capitalist market. While the term *liberatory* might be more easily articulated in the context of Freire's Brazilian peasants, critical scholars and teachers such as Giroux have not been shy about the need to liberate American college students from consumerism, from uncritical conformity, and from the unconscious reification of mainstream cultural ideology.

My argument is that if critical pedagogy is to be truly radical, its practitioners must offer more than just an alternative within the same political discourse; they must offer an alternative form of discourse. In fact, these oppositional formulations—that higher education should either serve to acculturate and normalize students or that it should serve to liberate and radicalize them—both gesture, it seems, to a social totality that lies at the horizon of some utopic social unity. In some sense, each *can* be accused of arguing that by following its path, society, at least as it is influenced by the institutions of higher education, will advance toward what social philosopher Ernesto Laclau calls "the destiny of the universal." In these gestures toward a totalized future, each formulation positions itself as a signpost to the true path of knowledge. The forces of cultural unity and tradition in the American educational system point to the need to acculturate and normalize the body politic under the universal ideas of national unity, Judeo-Christian morality, and cultural homogeneity, while the forces of liberation and radicalization point to the need to radicalize the body politic under the universal ideas of critique, identity politics, and resistance. The forces of the right point the way to a reconnection with "traditional values" where difference is eliminated and where the social body is united and univocal in its respect for specific moral values; the forces of the left point to a frontier where difference is valorized and where the sense of community is grounded in mutual respect and individual rights. What is clear is that neither position, at least as it is formulated strictly as an oppositional discourse, advances the argument much beyond a question of whose values should hold ideological hegemony within the academy. This is hardly the radical argument that is called for by the revolutionary ideas of social constructionism, poststructuralism, and the postmodern rhetorical turn.

What I argue here is that both views, while appearing to be incompatible, have come to be, in many ways, dependent on each other; they serve as two sides of the same coin. While the two goals for education would appear to be incompatible at some very basic levels, they are actually two dimensions of the same historical process, a process that probably only ensures the survival of the status quo. If critical teachers are to make real changes, then they may need to realize that as long as they construct their arguments in this way, their discourse *is* merely oppositional and not truly radical or revolutionary.

In fact, these positions both constitute what Laclau would call classic *emancipatory discourses*. Laclau argues that emancipatory discourses require this fundamental *dichotomic dimension* to operate, but that the dichotomy they set up is an illusion. The emancipatory project supposes an "absolute chasm, a radical discontinuity" between the "emancipatory moment and the social order which preceded it" (1), and requires that the past be constructed as a "radical other" which must be discarded if the subject is to be emancipated. In the rightist discourse of acculturation and national unity, this past is represented by the control (real or imagined) of the academy by the forces of radicalization and self-expression; in the leftist discourse of liberation, this past is represented by the control (real or imagined) of these same institutions by the forces of normalization and consumerism. What both of these discourses require to operate is what Laclau calls the "irreducible otherness of the oppressive system which is rejected" (4). This sets up a significant question about all discourses of emancipation:

> The alternative is clear: *either* emancipation is radical and, in that case, it has to be its own ground and confine what it excludes to a radical otherness constituted by evil or irrationality; *or* there is a deeper ground which establishes the rational connections between the pre-emancipatory order, the new "emancipated" one and the transition between both—in which case, emancipation cannot be considered as a truly *radical* foundation. (4)

In fact, I think that this is what is at the root of the failure of critical pedagogy to make more radical change than it has—even within the confines of the composition classroom. If it is constructed merely in opposition to traditional education, critical pedagogy will become (or perhaps has become) a form of institutionalized resistance which actually only supports the continuation of the status quo.[3] What is needed is a more postmodern notion of education.

Unfortunately, critical teachers who *have* attempted to embrace the postmodern turn have been accused of rejecting all universals and of promoting radical "particularism," and this criticism usually points to critical teachers' embrace of multiculturalism and "identity politics." Here, critical teachers are cited for valorizing relativist points of view or of promoting self expression in place of a unified sense of community. Indeed, even the move toward particularism is an appeal to a universal sense of emancipation, for if scholars and teachers of critical literacy and resistance pedagogy merely assert that students have a right to their own self-determination and that the institutions of higher education are generally in opposition to that goal, then they are in danger of merely reasserting that the right to self-determination is universally valid and that it is *that* value that will lead, finally, to a truly liberated society. This attitude can be seen, I think, in recent scholarship that has struggled with the dichotomies of *personal* and *public*, *individual* and *community*. This discussion indicates, I think, that critical pedagogy is dangerously close to becoming mired in endless discussions about what constitutes community, about whether community is constructed through negotiation or conflict, and about the relationship between the private and public spheres.

The postmodern perspective has arisen largely from a sense that the search for a set of universal values that can be applied to every situation is futile—that the formulation of universals, especially if they offer a unified sense of emancipation, generally lead to just the sort of paradoxical impasse that currently confronts scholars and teachers of critical literacy and critical pedagogy. How do we, then, rationalize our service to the mechanisms of ideological control and cultural normalization and, at the same time, empower and liberate our students as critical individuals?

Laclau points out that such paradoxes actually result from confusing the function of a universal with its content. He argues that universals can and should arise from the particulars of a hegemonic struggle, such as the one between traditional ideas of schooling and critical pedagogy, and that these universals make possible a "chain of equivalential effects" which serve to unite those involved in the hegemonic struggle under a universal that has no content of its own but that serves the function of bringing the parties together:

> If democracy is possible, it is because the universal has no necessary body and no necessary content; different groups, instead, compete between themselves to temporarily give to their particularisms a function of universal representation. Society generates a whole vocabulary of empty signifiers whose temporary signifieds are the result of a political competition. It is this final failure of society to constitute itself as society—which is the same thing as the failure of constituting difference as difference—which makes the distance between the universal and the particular unbridgeable and, as a result, burdens concrete social agents with the impossible task of making democratic interaction achievable. (35)

What this admittedly difficult passage suggests for the projects of critical pedagogy and resistance is this: if scholars and teachers of critical literacy and resistance pedagogy are to develop a discourse that is more than simply oppositional to the discourse of acculturation and service, they must somehow abandon their attachment to universal ideas of emancipation. Such a move would allow scholars and teachers of critical literacy and resistance pedagogy to join with students and with the academy in working toward a universalized horizon of social unity whose content is always deferred and whose identity is always constructed anew in each hegemonic context. What this means for scholars and teachers of critical literacy and resistance pedagogy is a decreased reliance on a self-portrayal that accents the oppositional nature of their discourse. It also suggest an increased awareness of how the content of the goals of critical literacy and pedagogy might resist becoming fixed within the traditions of emancipatory discourse and how they might rely, instead, on an increased employment of the deconstructive and historicizing strategies of the postmodern perspective.

By abandoning the discourse of emancipation, critical scholars and teachers might begin to turn away from the idea that any specific set of fixed practices can be trusted to liberate students or to create a unitary and utopic social totality. Instead, critical teachers might learn to allow a new set of universals to arise from each set of particular circumstances in the classroom, to resist fixing static ideas of critique and resistance into a discourse of emancipation, and to resist the idea that their theories and practices must always be constructed in opposition to the acculturative forces of higher education.

Hybridity and Empowering the Student

Much of the scholarship on critical literacy and critical pedagogy seems to end, as I have pointed out, in a call for student empowerment within the discourses of the academy and culture, and this is a call that I, too, have made in the previous chapters. Still, the nature of this empowerment has not been fully theorized, and attempts to empower students within the classroom under current theories of critical pedagogy have produced mixed results, as has been noted throughout this text. Critics of critical pedagogy have noted that attempts to empower students have too often relied on a fixed construction of what an empowered student would be—how he or she would act, think, and write—and how that student would view the world.

I have tried to suggest above that the universalist ideas of a critically empowered student can, and too often do, become merely the echo of modernity's exhausted master narrative of education as the emancipator of its subject. The alternative is to see that the goals of critical pedagogy can only be truly radical if they reject oppositional and emancipatory formulations. Instead of proposing a universalized idea of critique and resistance, critical scholars might emphasize the open and unformulated nature of an always empty and always deferred critical discursive ground, where students' and teachers' individual values and identities can be worked out in the intersubjectivity and intertextuality of postmodern notions of discourse and in the act of writing.

I see great possibility for a critical resistance that works against the notion that cultural, academic, and disciplinary discourses are fixed and rigid constructions that students must adapt themselves to in order to succeed. Such resistance would promote the idea—as it has been so succinctly articulated by Homi Bhabha, Gloria Anzaldúa, and other scholars of postcolonial theory—that writing is a mediation, or an intervention, into discourse and not merely a medium for ideas (Olson and Worsham 10). Each such intervention into discourse presences a new voice in the political din and forges a new hybrid text that rearticulates rhetoric in a new political space:

> The language of critique is effective not because it keeps forever separate the terms of the master and the slave, the mercantilist and the Marxist, but to the extent to which it overcomes the given grounds of opposition and opens up a space of translation: a place of hybridity, figuratively speaking, where the construction of a political object that is new, neither the one nor the other, properly alienates our political expectations and changes, as it must, the very forms of our recognition of the moment of politics. (*Locations* 25)

The question for critical scholars and teachers is not whether Freirean or neo-Marxist formulations of critical literacy can finally emancipate the subject, but whether we can face the possibility of such openings as Bhabha describes without rushing to fill them with our own political expectations and with our own need to replace contradiction with unity—whether we can help our students create the hybridized discourses they will need.

The concept of hybridized discourse, as it is described by Bhabha and other postcolonial theorists, is not about a mix of cultures; nor is it about a place where all ideas are magically given equal opportunity. Instead, it arises from the notion that it is hegemonic struggle itself that constitutes culture within the politics of a social democracy. Discourse, text, and rhetoric become sites where writers negotiate the spaces between their own values and the values of other writers in a way that exposes and critiques the power imbalances of that particular moment and space:

> Hybridization is really about how you negotiate between texts or cultures or practices in a situation of power imbalances in order to be able to see the way in which strategies of appropriation, revision, and iteration can produce possibilities for those who are less advantaged to be able to grasp in a moment of emergency, in the very process of the exchange or the negotiation, the advantage. (Olson and Worsham 39)

In the writing classroom, the idea of hybridization as it is expressed above offers critical teachers a moment in which they might abandon the project to emancipate and liberate students. By concerning ourselves with teaching students to see that their own writing is an intervention into academic and cultural discourse that reconjugates that discourse and that participates actively in the hegemonic struggle that constitutes the culture of social democracy then we might finally give real meaning to the project to empower them.

Resisting the Fixity of Discourse

Generally, scholars and teachers of critical pedagogy have spearheaded the project to politicize the classroom—a project that has finally cemented the relationship between culture, ideology, and rhetoric. As such, the projects of critical literacy and critical pedagogy have helped to reveal that rhetoric is always ideologically interested, that teaching is always political. More, these projects have helped reveal that the institutions of the academy are, from the beginning, politically interested and ideologically motivated. Most importantly, scholars and teachers of critical pedagogy have had the nerve to question those institutions and have helped to theorize the possibility that teachers and students might be empowered to resist dominant ideology—or at least its unquestioned acceptance—and to make English studies more than just a servant of acculturation and vocationalism.

In many ways, scholars and teachers of critical pedagogy have partaken of postmodern and poststructuralist philosophy in that they have embraced the revelation that the act of writing, in its broadest sense, is significant as the act in which subjects and groups may construct themselves and through which ideas and values enter into hegemonic struggle. Now, scholars and teachers of critical pedagogy face their biggest challenge. Critical pedagogy must take another step into the postmodern if it is to become more than an institutionalized opposition that serves merely to support the hegemony of dominant ideology in a perpetual dialogue of left versus right, individual versus society, and politics versus aesthetics. That step requires a commitment to teaching that discourse and rhetoric are open, available, dynamic, malleable, interested, and endlessly political. What must be resisted is the idea that discourses are fixed, rigid, and unavailable if English studies, and particularly rhetoric and composition, is to continue to constitute itself as a viable discipline. As it is, we are called upon more and more to address the seemingly irreconcilable goals of teaching students to critique and resist the unthinking acceptance of hegemonic values while at the same time providing them with the tools they need to succeed in the academy and in society. Scholars and teachers of critical pedagogy may yet lead the way—if we are brave enough to abandon our oppositional and emancipatory discourses and to truly embark on a radical project to empower ourselves and our students by learning and then teaching that writing is always an activity of resistance.

Notes

Chapter One
English Studies, Aestheticism,
and the Art-Culture System

1. One of the best brief histories, and one that demonstrates the problems with establishing an exact date for the beginnings of English studies, is Riley Parker's, "Where English Departments Come From."

2. Later, I will argue that understanding how definitions and concepts of culture have been historically defined is key to understanding current problems within English studies. Here, I follow the *American Heritage Dictionary*, which gives as its fifth definition of the word (after agricultural and biological uses) "the totality of socially transmitted behaviors, arts, beliefs, institutions, and all other products of human work and thought characteristic of a community or population."

3. Throughout, I follow the typical anthropological definition for *acculturation*, which is the process by which members of one culture adopt aspects of another, dominant culture as a result of contact and incorporation into a larger system. This word is contrasted with *enculturation*, which is used to mean the process by which members learn the rules and values of their own culture.

Chapter Two
Reproduction and Resistance

1. For a further discussion of Lu's theories about the use of conflict and resistance in writing instruction, see also, "Professing Multiculturalism," "From Silence to Words," and "Writing as Repositioning."

2. Unfortunately, it is this major difference in the two definitions of ideology that is conveniently left out of some critiques of the use of reproductive models. Reproductive models, as they are employed in cultural studies for instance, generally deploy Althusser's more complex and generous concept of ideology. Using this construction, students are not usually seen as intellectually naive victims who are suffering under a veil of false consciousness, but as active, aware participants in classroom practices that highlight the contestatory, dialogic "working-out" of values within the representations and practices of popular texts and institutions.

Chapter Three
Ethics and the Writing Class

1. Popular thought has done much to problematize notions of just what constitutes *the postmodern* and the terms in which it is presented. I will defer specifically to Lyotard, who has objected to the use of both the terms *postmodern theory* and *postmodernism*. Lyotard has pointed out that the postmodern perspective is neither a *theory* nor an *ism*. As such, I prefer to use *the postmodern, postmodernity*, or, more often, the *postmodern perspective*.

2. These theorists cover a wide variety of topics in their work, and this listing should not be viewed as the reduction of what is actually a huge and varied volume of thought to one consensual promotion of the postmodern perspective or to the constructionist view of language. However, each of these theorists, in his own way, has contributed to the notion that language works to construct our conception of reality and that the "real" is only known as it is mediated through language. What I hope to imply by this list is the shear volume of writing that has produced the idea that language mediates our vision of reality.

3. I am becoming increasingly convinced that because students are already fairly good at "reading" cultural texts, cultural studies has an important place in the composition class. Students often have experience reading advertisements, popular film, and song lyrics that rivals that of the best-informed teacher, and their facility in discussing the details of these texts can be employed to promote an initial awareness of the interested nature of discourse. Nevertheless, as I argue in Chapter One, the project of critical literacy is most aptly served by the elimination of the distinction between "cultural" texts and "literary" texts.

4. Interestingly, these European scholars have largely complained that the postmodern perspective usually associated with them is something that is discussed primarily by American scholars. Derrida, Lyotard, and others who have been associated with the postmodern perspective have, at times, totally dissociated themselves from any mention of the postmodern. Lyotard has addressed the subject most directly. At times he seems almost to see it as his place to explain the postmodern perspective even as he denies its viability.

Chapter Four
Subjects and Power

1. I would also include the work of Min-Zhan Lu, Bruce Horner, and Morris Young in the list of scholars who have been particularly interested in issues of authority in the classroom and who have built upon the work of critical literacy to begin a reconsideration of the political nature of classroom authority. I have discussed some of their work in earlier chapters, but I wish to indicate that it is pertinent to this discussion, too.

2. For an interesting account of how this type of realignment was tried at the Stanford University, read Mary Louis Pratt's "Humanities for the Future: Reflections on the Western Culture Debate at Stanford."

3. It may be tempting at times to read my critique of cultural studies as harsher than I intend. I believe that cultural studies does, in fact, turn the attention of classes toward issues of production, as I have stated earlier. In this way, cultural studies, does, in fact, contribute to

the project to politicize the classroom—especially as it addresses the way in which certain texts and conventions of reading and writing are evaluated within the academy and within the classroom.

Chapter Five
Resistance, Emancipation, and Hybridity

1. Ironically, the fact that critical pedagogy promotes self-reflexive critique and self-disclosure on the part of the teacher or researcher means that critical teachers are just as likely to report their failures as they are to report their successes.

2. For an example of Freire's responses to these criticisms, see Gary A. Olson's interview with Friere "History, *Praxis*, and Change: Paulo Freire and the Politics of Literacy."

3. It also may be useful to remember here that resistance that operates from formulations of oppressed and oppressor primarily serves to reinscribe those very structures.

Works Cited

Arnold, Matthew. *Culture and Anarchy.* (1932). Cambridge: Cambridge UP, 1957.

——. *"From* The Function of Criticism at the Present Time." (1865) *The Norton Anthology of English Literature.* Ed. M. H. Abrams. 6th ed. 2 vols. New York: Norton, 1993: 1389-403.

Aronowitz, Stanley, and Henry Giroux. *Education Still Under Siege.* Westport: Bergin, 1993.

——. *Postmodern Education: Politics, Culture, and Social Criticism.* Minneapolis: U of Minnesota P, 1991.

Bauman, Zygmunt. *Postmodern Ethics.* Cambridge: Blackwell, 1994.

Berlin, James A. Introduction. Berlin, *Rhetoric* ii-xxi.

——. "Composition and Cultural Studies." Hurlbert and Blitz, *Composition* 47-55.

——. "Rhetoric and Ideology in the Writing Class." *College English* 50 (1988): 477-94.

——. *Rhetorics, Poetics, and Cultures: Refiguring College English Studies.* Urbana: NCTE, 1996.

119

——. *Writing Instruction in Nineteenth-Century American Colleges*. Carbondale: Southern Illinois UP, 1984.

Bhabha, Homi K. *The Location of Culture*. New York: Routledge, 1994.

Bizzell, Patricia. *Academic Discourse and Critical Consciousness*. Pittsburgh: U of Pittsburgh P, 1992.

Bourdieu, Pierre, and Jean-Claude Passeron. *Reproduction in Education, Society and Culture*. Beverly Hills: Sage, 1977.

Brooke, Robert. "Underlife and Writing Instruction." *College Composition and Communication* 38 (1987): 141-53.

Buffington, Nancy, and Clyde Moneyhun. "A Conversation with Gerald Graff and Ira Shor." *JAC: A Journal of Composition Theory* 17 (1997): 1-21.

Clifford, James. "On Collecting Art and Culture." During 49-73.

Connors, Robert J. *Composition-Rhetoric: Backgrounds, Theory, and Pedagogy*. Pittsburgh: U of Pittsburgh P, 1997.

Crowley, Sharon. *A Teacher's Introduction to Deconstruction*. Urbana: NCTE, 1989.

Dean, Terry. "Multicultural Classrooms, Monocultural Teachers." *College Composition and Communication* 40 (1989): 23-37.

Dobrin, Sidney I. *Constructing Knowledges: The Politics of Theory-Building in Composition*. Albany: State U of New York P, 1997.

——. "English Departments and the Question of Disciplinarity." Rev. of *What is English Teaching*, by Chris Davies, *A Teaching Subject*, by Joe Harris, and *English as a Discipline*, by James C. Raymond. *College English* 59 (1997): 692-99.

During, Simon, ed. *The Cultural Studies Reader*. New York: Routledge, 1993.

Eagleton, Terry. *Ideology: An Introduction.* London: Verso, 1991.

——. *Literary Theory: An Introduction.* Minneapolis: U of Minnesota P, 1996.

Edelstein, Marilyn. "Toward a Feminist Postmodern Poléthique: Kristeva on Ethics and Politics." *Ethics, Politics, and Difference in Julia Kristeva's Writing.* Ed. Kelly Oliver. New York: Routledge, 1993. 196-214.

Fish, Stanley. *Professional Correctness: Literary Studies and Political Change.* Oxford: Clarendon, 1995.

Foucault, Michel. "Truth and Power." *The Foucault Reader.* Ed. Paul Rabinow. New York: Pantheon, 1984. 51-75.

——. "What is an Author?" *Contemporary Literary Criticism: Literary and Cultural Studies.* 3rd ed. Ed. Davis and Schleifer. New York: Longman, 1997.

Gale, Xin-Liu. *Teachers, Discourses, and Authority in the Postmodern Composition Classroom.* Albany: State U of New York P, 1996.

Giroux, Henry. "Where Have All the Public Intellectuals Gone? Racial Politics, Pedagogy, and Disposable Youth." *JAC: A Journal of Composition Theory* 17 (1997): 191-205.

Goleman, Judith. *Working Theory: Critical Composition Studies for Students and Teachers.* Westport: Bergin, 1995.

Greenbaum, Andrea. "'Every Difference Will Be Used Against Us': An Interview with Ira Shor." *Writing on the Edge* 8 (1997): 7-20.

Hardin, Joe Marshall. Rev. of *When Students Have Power: Negotiating Authority in a Critical Pedagogy*, by Ira Shor. *JAC: A Journal of Composition Theory* 17 (1997): 525-29.

Harris, Joseph. "Negotiating the Contact Zone." *Journal of Basic Writing* 14 (1995): 27-42.

Harris, Joseph, and Jay Rosen. "Teaching Writing as Cultural Criticism." Hurlbert and Blitz, *Composition* 58-68.

Horner, Bruce. "Students, Authorship, and the Work of Composition." *College English* 59 (1997): 505-29.

Hurlbert, C. Mark, and Michael Blitz. "An Uncomfortable State of Mind." Hurlbert and Blitz, *Composition* 43-46.

——, eds. *Composition and Resistance.* Portsmouth: Heineman, 1991.

——. "Resisting Composure." Hurlbert and Blitz, *Composition* 1-5.

Knoblauch, C. H. "Critical Teaching and Dominant Culture." Hurlbert and Blitz, *Composition* 12-21.

Kristeva, Julia. "The Ethics of Linguistics." *Desire in Language.* Ed. Leon Roudiez. New York: Columbia UP, 1980.

Laclau, Ernesto. *Emancipations.* NY: Verso, 1996.

Lu, Min-Zhan. "Conflict and Struggle: The Enemies or Preconditions of Basic Writing." *College English* 54 (1992): 887-913.

Lyotard, Jean-François. The *Differend: Phrases in Dispute.* Trans. George van den Abbeele. Minneapolis: U of Minnesota P, 1988.

——. "Defining the Postmodern." During 170-73.

Lyotard, Jean-François, and Jean-Loup Thébaud. *Just Gaming.* Trans. Wlad Godzich. Minneapolis: U of Minnesota P, 1985.

McCance, Dawn. *Posts: Re Addressing the Ethical.* Albany: State U of New York P, 1996.

Merod, Jim. *The Political Responsibility of the Critic.* NY: Cornell UP, 1987.

Miller, Richard E. "The Arts of Complicity: Pragmatism and the Culture of Schooling."College English 61 (1998): 10-28.

Miller, Susan. *Rescuing the Subject: A Critical Introduction to Rhetoric and the Writer.* Carbondale: Southern Illinois UP, 1991.

——. *Textual Carnivals: The Politics of Composition.* Carbondale: Southern Illinois UP, 1991.

Miraglia, Eric. "Resistance and the Writing Teacher." *JAC: A Journal of Composition Theory* 17 (1997): 415-35.

Olson, Gary A. "Encountering the Other: Postcolonial Theory and Composition Scholarship." *Journal of Advanced Composition* 18 (1998): 45-55.

——. "History, Praxis, and Change: Paulo Friere and the Politics of Literacy." Olson and Gale 153-68.

——. "Jacques Derrida on Rhetoric and Composition." Olson and Gale 121-41.

——. "Resisting a Discourse of Mastery: A Conversation with Jean-François Lyotard." *Women, Writing, Culture.* Ed. Gary A. Olson and Elizabeth Hirsh. Albany: State U of New York P, 1995. 169-92.

Olson, Gary A., and Irene Gale, eds. *(Inter)views: Cross-Disciplinary Perspectives on Rhetoric and Literacy.* Edwardsville: Southern Illinois UP, 1991.

Olson, Gary A., and Lynn Worsham. "Staging the Politics of Difference: Homi Bhabha's Critical Literacy." *Race, Rhetoric, and the Postcolonial.* Ed. Gary A. Olson and Lynn Worsham. Albany: State U of New York P, 1999. 3-39.

Parker, William Riley. "Where Do English Departments Come From?" *College English* 28 (1967): 339-51.

Pratt, Mary Louise. "Humanities for the Future: Reflections on the Western Culture Debate at Stanford." *Intellectuals: Aesthetics, Politics, Academics.* Ed. Bruce Robbins. Minneapolis: U of Minnesota P, 1990. 13-31.

Porter, James E. "Developing a Postmodern Ethics of Rhetoric and Composition." *Defining the New Rhetorics*. Ed. Theresa Enos and Stuart C. Brown. Newbury Park, CA: Sage, 1993. 207-26.

Rorty, Richard. *Philosophy and the Mirror of Nature*. Princeton, NJ: Princeton UP, 1979.

Russell, David R. *Writing in the Academic Discipline, 1870-1990: A Curricular History*. Carbondale: Southern Illinois UP, 1991.

Sledd, James. "How We Apples Swim." Hurlbert and Blitz 145-49.

Smith, Jeff. "Student's Goals, Gatekeeping, and Ethics," *College English* 59 (1997): 299-320.

Stotsky, Sandra. "Conceptualizing Writing as Moral and Civic Thinking." *College English* 54 (1992): 27-56.

Tobin, Lad. "Reading Students, Reading Ourselves: Revising the Teacher's Role in the Writing Class." *College English* 53 (1991): 333-48.

Tuman, Myron. "From Astor Place to Kenyon Road: The NCTE and the Origins of English Studies." *College English* 48 (1986): 339-49.

Turner, Graeme. *British Cultural Studies: An Introduction*. New York: Routledge, 1990.

Watkins, Evan. *Work Time: English Departments and the Circulation of Cultural Value*. Stanford: Stanford UP, 1989.

Williams, Raymond. *Keywords: A Vocabulary of Culture and Society*. New York: Oxford UP, 1976.

Young, Morris. "Narratives of Identity: Theorizing the Writer and the Nation." *Journal of Basic Writing* 15 (1996): 50-75.

Index